PURPOSE DRIVEN MARRIAGE

God's Purpose Drives A Marriage For A Lifetime

Dr. Paul Obadare and Dr. Myrna Etheridge

AuthorHouse™
1663 Liberty Drive
Bloomington, IN 47403
www.authorhouse.com
Phone: 1-800-839-8640

Names and places within illustrations are fictitious to
provide protection for individuals. Please, do not feel singled
out—you were not. Illustrations are compilations.

© 2009 Dr. Paul Obadare and Dr. Myrna Etheridge. All rights reserved.

No part of this book may be reproduced, stored in retrieval system, or
transmitted by any means without the written permission of the author.

First published by AuthorHouse 10/28/2009
ISBN: 978-1-4490-3564-8 (e)
ISBN: 978-1-4490-3563-1 (sc)

Library of Congress Control Number: 2009910783

Unless otherwise identified, all Scripture quotations
are from the New King James Version of the Bible.
All emphases are added by the author.

Verses marked AMP are taken from the Amplified Bible,
© The Lockman Foundation, 1954, 1958 (New Testament),
© Zondervan Publishing House, 1962, 1964 (Old Testament).

Verses marked NAS are taken from the New American Standard Bible,
© Lockman Foundation, 1960, 1962, 1963, 1968, 1972, and 1973.

Printed in the United States of America
Bloomington, Indiana

This book is printed on acid-free paper.

TABLE OF CONTENTS

PART I INTRODUCTION

Chaper 1: Introduction	3
Chapter 2: Marriage as an Investment	6
Children—Wasted Investments	9
Cars/Houses—Wasted Investments	11
Chapter 3: Marriage Is a Union	15

PART II THE ANACHRONISM OF MARRIAGE

Chapter 4: Man: Image & Meaning	23
Chapter 5: Appreciation	33
Chapter 6: Respect	44
Respect is Commanded in the Bible	52
What Respect is	52
Chapter 7: Responsability	61
Husband's Role and Purposes in Marriage	63
Woman's Role and Purpose in Marriage	68
Chapter 8: Intimacy in Marriage	83
Chapter 9: Accountability	92

Accountability Summed Up	94
Chapter 10: Giving	100
Chapter 11: Enduring Eternal Relationship	108

PART III APPLYING THE IDEAL PURPOSE TO LIFE AND THE ORDEAL OF SIN

Chapter 12: Functions of Repentance	123
The Effects of Sin Ended Your Marriage	124
Chapter 13: Mercy and Grace for Marriages	129
Chapter 14: Avoiding the Enduring Effects of Failed Marriage	134
Change to Rejoin God's Purpose	137
Chapter 15: Avoiding the Enduring Effects of Divorce	140
Chapter 16: The Grace to be Single or Begin Again	147
Dr. Grady Lloyd Etheridge, Ph.BD, DD., MB, BA,	154
ABOUT THE AUTHORS	160
Dr. Paul Obadare, Ph.D., Dr. C, SCC, MRS, BA in Religious Studies	160
Dr. Myrna L. Etheridge, Ph.D., D.D., D.D., MSE, BSE	162
COMBINED BENEFITS OF THE AUTHORS	164

PART I

INTRODUCTION

Chapter 1

Introduction

Know about a divinely unique and strategically orchestrated institution? It's marriage. The original Goal of Marriage was for facilitation of communication. Community relationship was the Purpose of Marriage. The end result of marriage was both divine and earthly. It was designed by God to implement and create an enjoyable, secure relationship which contained compulsory enforcements to safeguard the family. This type of community unit was necessary for expansion of mankind.

God created mankind in his own image to insure and secure communication between Him and His creation. He desires to have the work of His hands communicate with Him in a special way. Although the formation of the angelic world was not made known to us, we are well aware that, since creation, the maker, designer of man has been talking to man. Man was created in His divine image. Communication is an exchange device necessary for meaningful existence and for enhancing vitality of being alive. Without communication, there is no real life. Thus, man was created to exchange ideas, thoughts, intentions, emotions, etc, with his maker.

Purpose Driven Marriage

Likewise woman, whom God fashioned, created, or made out of man's bones was to give meaning to his life through communication with him as her husband.

God did not make man only for interaction, but also to have fellowship with Him in an atmosphere of community affairs. His intention was to have a holy community of people with unique adorable differences—colors, languages, customs, etc. God's creations were fashioned to interrelate; that is, to interact with each other in a spiritual way. That relationship could then reflect and operate bringing forth His glory.

Finally, our belief is that the divine finality—or the end result of His creation—was to bless this creation benefiting it through numerical expansion. Procreation, enlargement, and filling the earth, became compulsory for His creation.

God was creating mankind to occupy and possess His natural world. Man was to pro-create and multiply. The working design of the creator, and His command for man was to occupy—even the universe. Man became the carrier of the divine image and spiritual importance of Jehovah God to the entire "world" and all His creation.

Man was to explore the works of creation and enjoy them. Thus, marriage is divinely intended to manage God's determined expansion program of His image in this world, called the "earth."

Consider the letters that compose the word "Marriage." Contained within these letters of one important word, we believe are volumes of meaning. This book will use these letters individually to expatiate, amplify and expound on the divine meaning of the word "Marriage."

God's Purpose Drives A Marriage For A Lifetime

One reader commented: "This book would be good for couples who are engaged or those seeking engagement. It needs to be studied and implemented. It gives purpose. Others, as I am would have a difficult time trying to implement this after being married a long time. If one partner is unwilling to change, or the marriage has been very hard so that walls are built it would be an uphill job. With God's help all things are possible, so there is hope even when years have been very hard and your partner wants you to do all the changing." (LJ from IL)

Summary:
- ➤ The purpose of man's creation was for fellowship, community and a creative environment for numerical increase and the nurturing of children.
- ➤ God desired to communicate with mankind and share in the creative work in the setting on earth.
- ➤ God's meaningful creation of man was to facilitate communication with the uniquely created couple—in His own image.
- ➤ Man's commission and design plan calls him to occupy the world and be productive while enjoying the creations.
- ➤ Marriage was to establish on earth the same kind of unity and cooperation as was patterned by God's divinity trinity union.

Questions to Focus on Chapter 1 Insight:
1. What primary purpose was the original Goal of Marriage?
2. What is communication?
3. Why did God need communication?
4. The goal for the community of people was?
5. Man was to carry a message to the world. What was it?

Chapter 2

Marriage as an Investment

God's only reason for considering or meeting our desire is an outward flow of His great love and mercy! How great is His love.

God's love is toward us, even when we make and are in our sinful choices. His love is never in relation to or based upon a reference to our qualifications. He loves because He created and gave life to us. You can't earn this love. Neither can you make it go away!

It is unearned and enduring, love devoted to you from your creator-designer. His love for you is just because you are. We repeat, you could never earn it nor do you deserve it! Take a couple of days to think on that! Meditate further on the intentions from John 3: 16-18. "For God so loved the world that He sent His only begotten son…"

In its final essence, and ideal flow of marriage love equals the purpose displayed on earth for the example of the Father-Son-Holy Spirit's valuable, pure unity. This is opposite of what we will term "Wasted Investments."

God's Purpose Drives A Marriage For A Lifetime

When we look at marriage like the Genesis 1:1-2 account of creation we begin to see the parallel of the eternal home to our home's reality. There was such connectedness between the intent of the Father, the Word of the Son and the action of the Holy Spirit.

Before the command over the face of the deep, there was no order, no life, and no meaningful existence for the earth. The Holy Spirit moved, brooded, began stirring the potential of the earth and the darkness and void (unordered raw materials) where changed and God's kind of life—light—love came upon the earth.

"In the beginning God created the heavens and the earth. The earth was (became) without form, and void; and darkness was on the face of the deep. And the Spirit of God was hovering (brooding) over the face of the waters. Then God said, "Let there be light; and there was light." Genesis 1:1-3 NKJV

With that first day, order arrived into the world and God said it was good. When He ordered the design for His creation His character was shown. When God's orderly, meaningful design is not involved in our marriages we will not find that good. We will only find "Wasted Investments."

MARRIAGE—WASTED INVESTMENTS

Marriages not based on Godly values, and His system, are wasted investments. Ones based upon material satisfactions, psychological mental hypes, societal dictations, borrowed Western or Eastern proliferated ideologies, new age knowledge or intelligence all end in wasted investments!

The fear, knowledge and awareness of God, value of unity and true joy have been born out of all these stereotype systems. So, when a family wants to base healthy relationships on these vain ideas and faulty learning, the family wastes their valuable investment. It is like dumping treasures into a city drain sewer or pouring water into a basket or bucket with holes that hold no valuable water!

This is at the root and causes confusions, pains, disorientations, dissatisfactions, destabilization, and destruction in today's families.

The world system controlled by the devil has completely changed the value of today's family to glamorize vanity. He deceived them into believing that there is peace in what they do (their work), and power in what they are called (their title). In this way, power, satisfaction and greed have become the value system in today's family structure. This is what we're terming wasted investment.

Many families invest heavily in making their family mentally healthy by providing material satisfaction to the family. However, the wine of romance and love soon dry up when there are no fulfillments or satisfactions in the investments. They are "down the drain" so to speak, when the marriage ends in separation or collapses in divorce. At this point each partner and the children are forced to start all over again with a new family. How or whatever they end up with is sometimes deadly. The husband may kill the wife and children or vice versa. All of their labor and treasures end in wasted investments.

CHILDREN—WASTED INVESTMENTS

Many parents whether they be Eastern, Western or World dwellers, invest heavily in their children. Numerous, especially in the west, believe in taking good care of their children. They invest in education (with loans), purchase big houses (the children need the space), provide expensive toys (to stimulate their young minds), take them on expensive trips (to expand their knowledge of the world); and, give them the best educations (for status and because their children are brighter than they are).

You ask, "What is the end result of all these investments?"

Their work ends in waste because they reared the children without a foundation of Godly values based on Godly principles. All their energy, time and resources become wasted investments. These parents did not train their children in the ways of God. They failed to lead the children to fear God. They failed to educate their children to live a righteous life. Some have no knowledge of God at all! Others claim they are Christians but without evidence of a changed heart.

The children, after using up all the parental investments, leave their parent's houses without looking back. They have no thought or care for their parents. They have become expert in living as they were taught: live for yourself. They are totally selfish in their life style. In the future they end up sending their parents to nursing homes and may visit them once in a while. Some wait for their parents to die so the inheritance will come into their hands. Others even kill parents before their time to collect family money. What wasted investments! They are investments without returns.

Children in some instances, because of wrong family values give birth to untimely children. They leave this child's care as an enormous responsibility and liability to their parents or their grandparents. These "mistake" children are dumped into the laps of tired parents without a thank you or thought. What wasted investments.

The end result of all this parental care for the children will most likely become that the parents face a nursing home and a lack of loving care. There are no returns from these investments, just abandonments and desertions. In order for children to live long lives and avoid curses, they are Biblically mandated to care for parents who have need or for ones who have grown old needing care and support.

Parents, who are loved, are encouraged to move into their child's home so they may receive care and live healthy lives. This prolongs life and prevents loneliness. They live in warmly accorded, adequate care and comfort. Parents need protection and provision. Although some of the aged are wealthy, they still really need love and comfort. Think about it, these parents took time to care for their child's discomforts, liabilities and troubles while the children were young. No matter the condition of the parent—sick, healthy, poor or rich—it is the children's duty to insure parents live with them giving proper and comforting care to their parents.

When parents are old, they may need help. Then comes the opportunity to invest your time and energy on their behalf. If you choose not to give this care you will be a wasted investment to your parents.

Cars/Houses—Wasted Investments

If an automobile or dwelling is the priority of a family, they are wasted investments before God. Anything embraced without making God the first priority and having Him as the family's head, is a wasted investment.

A job without acknowledging its giver (God) will end abruptly. The employment either ends by termination or closure of the business. If it is a vehicle, it will end either in an accident, through repossession, or as a debt because of constant need for repairs and replacement costs.

If the emphasis is on an impressive house, sometimes it becomes an attraction for a robber. That may mean there is a resultant theft, insecurity or even death. Some may be repossessed (because they were too expensive for the family budget), lost in court battles, or lost because of bad financial decisions.

If a business was started without giving God credit, after many years of operation and work it either ends in foreclosure or ends up in someone's hands that live outside God's blessings. They have no clue about its beginnings. So, where are the investments? When a business is started without God's principles; it ends as a wasted investment.

Purpose Driven Marriage

Marriage—Of what value is your investment?

Pause for a moment and ask yourself, "Where is this marriage investment going to end?" What will be the outcome of this investment? What are the priorities of our family investments? What dictates the values of this home? What are the sources of our real treasures? What is the basis for the value system? Which culture is shaping and molding this family? What hopes and decisions do we hold to insure bringing up Godly children? Are the investments in our children secured in God? Will they bring peaceful and fruitful returns when we are old or in need? Are we really well known by our mate or children? Do we really know them? If these questions are too difficult to answer, stop right now and seek help! If God's principles are not the values in your home; if He doesn't control your life—you are simply investing into nothing but losses—wasted investments!

Many Christians serve God but they really don't know Him. They are filled with worthwhile responsibilities, activities and actions, yet, soon they discover their services and giving are wasted investments. These Christians fail to obey the principles of Christ given in His word (Bible). They refuse to take on the nature of the Christ they proclaim. The knowledge of Jesus is not found in hypocrisy and falsehood. Many Christian homes are ending in divorce and bitter separations because Godly awe and principles portrayed in the life of Christ are difficult for them to put into practice. What doubly wasted investments.

This has probably seemed an aggressive, upsetting series of conclusions. There will be no way to have a value filled marriage investment without Jesus being accorded the proper position as the head of our marriages. Please, accept this as the best advice we have to challenge you to stop investing in efforts that will bring no increase. There is much to say for the value of marriage that is based upon the headship of God. Keep reading—your marriage investment is worth the effort.

Summary:
- God's love radiates to man even when he was not deserving or qualified.
- Man could never earn God's love, yet He loves man relentlessly.
- Marriage when it is enlarged to God's design displays the Father-Son-Spirit unity on earth.
- Without the orderly meaningful design God intended, marriage will not seem "good."
- "Wasted Investments" result from investing in education, mental growth, world's ways, indulging children's whims.
- The marriage patterned by God's divinity trinity union never produces "wasted investments."
- Without truly knowing God and having Jesus as the head of the family, no marriage can become the joyful relationship God intended. Honoring and loving God is central to avoiding "wasted investments."

Questions to Focus on Chapter 2 Insight:
1. What was the motivation for God to respond to our desires?
2. How can God's love be displayed on the earth?
3. What are some areas that will result in "wasted investments" when Godly principles and knowing God are neglected?
4. How do others perceive your marriage? Probably they look at things on the outside, right? What about the things on the inside?

5. When parents are not honored by their children what is probably happening in the home?
6. A lack of love and knowledge of God could result in what?

Chapter 3

Marriage Is a Union

Marriage is a functional unit formed between a man and a woman in a covenanted, permanent relationship. Marriage is part of God's intention for humanity from creation. It forms the basis for the family, which is the primary unit of society. Where marriage flourishes both the couples and the whole communities are blessed.

This institution is the basic foundation of any healthy community. When this institution is destroyed, the basic foundation of God's solution for His creation is destroyed. When marriage fails, society fails, becoming meaningless and valueless.

Marriage first of all is a covenant-relationship between two individuals, husband—male, and wife—female. One is the stronger, offering protection, more stability in reasoning, and with authority. The other—the wife—is weaker (more vulnerable to attack) when pregnant with young; in general she lacks brute male strength physically, and mentally she was able to be deceived. She was gullible when satan tempted her repeatedly.

Purpose Driven Marriage

"When he arose, he took the young child and his mother by night, and departing into Egypt" Matthew 2:14.

Notice, Joseph took Mary and left for Egypt. That was his decision to obey God's direction. The role of the husband is like that. As the Father God stated over Israel,."…I spread my skirt over you, and covered thy nakedness: yea, I swore unto thee, and entered into a covenant with thee, says the LORD GOD, and thou became mine. I washed… I clothed… I girded…I decked thee with ornaments… gold, jewel, crown…And thy renown went forth among the heathen for thy beauty: for it was perfect through my comeliness, which I had put upon thee, says the LORD GOD" Ezekiel 16:8-14.

The Ezekiel passage describes the important role of a covenant-relationship. This relationship goes deep into our mental being and holds us even more strongly in our fleshly union. The result should be it keeps one committed to the other for a lifetime.

"And Adam was not deceived, but the woman being deceived was in the transgression. Notwithstanding she shall be saved in childbearing, if they continue in faith and charity and holiness with sobriety" I Timothy 2:14.

"To deliver thee from the strange woman, even from the stranger, who flatters with her words; which forsakes the guide of her youth, and forget the covenant of her God. For, her house inclines unto death, and her paths unto the dead. That thou may walk in the way of good men, and keep the paths of the righteous." Proverbs 2:16-19. KJV

From creation according to God's pattern He made masculine—feminine character (Genesis 1:27). They are designed to complement each other and become a bonded one-flesh unit in marriage, so much so that the man leaves his father and mother and cleaves to his wife (Matthew 19:4). The bonding of man and wife is God's design and is a unit that God puts together. He establishes a marriage bond—"NO HUMAN, God's Word says, is to cause problems such that the bonded ones are separated" (Mark 10:6).

Women who are married are to respect their husbands—showing honor and remembering they are to be the "crowning glory" of their own husband. She is to reflect his being, represent his manhood, and enjoy his companionship. Woman was created for man—so she is created able to skillfully adapt to her mate and should. If she does not honor her husband she may expect eminent problems, because of the enemy's fallen angels. THEY WILL ATTACK HER! She will be exposed by her unwillingness to honor, submit (give honor and respect) to her husband (I Corinthians 11:11-12). The larger passage is verses 7-16. The husband has great responsibilities for protection, care and provision for his mate. There are qualities missing when a man and woman are independent of each other. In verse twelve they are one in everything. They are flowing from each other, and inter-dependent. When each contributes the result is gaining completeness and wholeness.

Marriage therefore is to provide:

Companionship—She is a helpmate—counselor, one alongside, helper, and in-his-face friend who may be trusted to faithfully keep her mate's best interests in focus (Genesis 2:18; 2:20-22; 3:12; Proverbs 31:10-12).

Purpose Driven Marriage

Commitment—It is to be an exclusive relationship where the husband loves the wife and she respects him! He decides to love her and she determines to respect him and show honor throughout life (Genesis 2:23-24; Mark 10:7-8; I Corinthians 7:2; Ephesians 5:31).

Lifelong partnership—Only death ends the Godly marriage. Everyone who is not gifted to live without marriage needs to have their own marriage partner so they will not be tempted to sin sexually. After a mate dies it will still be best to remain single, but to marry in the Lord is permitted (Romans 7:2, I Corinthians 7:27-29, 39-40).

Procreation—It is the intended atmosphere for procreation and rearing children. The seed was to be protected and led to the Lord by the believing mate. And in marriage, a husband was to be honest and openly faithful to the wife of his youth (Malachi 2:15, I Corinthians 7:14-15).

Limitation--Marriage is limited to and exists for affairs of this world. It will not exist in the world to come—Jesus said in the world to come they will neither marry nor give in marriage, but will be as the angels—no marriages. The fashion of this world will pass away. The corporate Christ will become the unified body united in Heavenly love. Marriage on earth was to have the pattern of the Heavenly love bond—love elevated to divine love (Matthew 22:30, Luke 20:34-35; I Corinthians 7:29-31).

Be reminded this book's intent is to reveal the purposes which drive, propel, or give the power needed to keep marriage vital. To accomplish this we will expand and expound upon words beginning with the letters that comprise the word "Marriage." It is my belief that manifold volumes could be used with marriage as an anachronism before all the meanings that empower growing marriages might be explored to their fullest.

The Part II of Purpose Driven Marriage will use—within reason—ample divine meanings to show God's plan for each letter's selected word.

"Marriage" expanded becomes God's illustrated message for man to use as an empowered step by step pattern for becoming more like Himself. Marriage can be driven by these purposes! The process is so invigorating that the life time bond will seem only days long.

Summary:
- The primary unit of society is marriage. It is between a man and his wife.
- Marriage is the only blood covenant that is widely used in today's society and it is designed to last a lifetime.
- Healthy community depends upon healthy marriage.
- A husband's duty is to protect, provide for and tend to his wife to insure the continuation of mankind upon the earth. Without this support the woman would be in danger physically during pregnancy and during decision making times.
- Woman's greatest weakness is that she can be deceived—rather easily.
- The man was to leave his parents and cling to the wife.
- Women are to respect their husband and honor him.
- A husband who doesn't listen to his wife is devoid of his best advisor.
- Marriage is a world system. It will not exist in Heaven. The power of married love will propel

Purpose Driven Marriage

and give power to human love and reveal God's purposes.

Questions to Focus on Chapter 3 Insight:
1. Why can marriage function on earth, but not be necessary in Heaven?
2. The marriage relationship is one based upon intimate exchange both mentally, emotionally and physically. Why did God talk about Israel like a husband would toward his wife?
3. A service to the husband is the watchfulness of a devoted wife to fend off advances or potential harm to their relationship from other persons. How does she do this?
4. Being masculine or femine is good and adds meaning to relationship. In what ways to the different traits strengthen marriage?
5. What does a companion do?
6. What is an anachronism?

PART II

THE ANACHRONISM OF MARRIAGE

Chapter 4

Man: Image & Meaning

M—represents my meaningful image.

The world was chaotic without the presence of God. The Bible said the natural world was in darkness and the spirit of the Lord had no residence but was brooding over the surface of the waters. No meaning existed in that lifeless world until the Lord visited the earth and carried out His provision to change the situation. To change this "stand still" world, meaning had to be created. This began the formation of lights and the daily systematic creation of the world. God first made the world meaningful. He continues to create the kinds of creatures and their specific functions. He separated them and gave them boundaries. God made meaning out of the void earth: He applied His purpose.

To understand and fathom the purpose of the meaningful image God created is to know who God is. We would not have had the opportunity of knowing about the existence of God without our own existence. God concluded his creation (Genesis 1:26-27) by creating using His pattern, Elohim, his own replica; that is, His own image through the formation of man. God made the natural world appear. The plant and animal kingdoms all display His unsearchable wisdom and infinite being. But nothing was meaningful to Him in them until He made His own "carbon copy", man.

God said, "Let Us make man in Our own image." In other words, let Me make one having Our own image that would give meaning to Our image.

The world without man was void, without meaning. The angelic beings may have had the opportunity of knowing God, but man could not have known of God without his own origin by creation, neither could God have mattered without man.

To the human race we declare: God created His own image so as to make His own world meaningful to Himself. Man is God made. Man is His likeness, image, resemblance, duplicate, glory, feelings and nature. Man is truly a finite copy of the infinite God.

Humankind is the exact image of God spiritually. Man is a spiritual being, a house of mud. The flesh is from the earth. We call the mud house human flesh. Man is the mobile temple of God. All the nature of God is reproduced in man. This is why redemption was important. God came to this world, limited to the same form as man, to redeem His original image. It had been damaged by the fallen angel, the devil.

This imputed value is what makes man special. The work of Jesus, marred by sin in the world, perfected the work of image repairer and image restorer for man. The image of God cannot be destroyed by His own created being, the devil. God created the devil and his helpers who became rebels (or were commanded by their boss, the devil) after the devil's choice to rebel.

Review the reasons behind God's revealing purpose: Satan can't create anything. Man became the meaning of the natural world. When man was created, the work of God took on meaning, order, delight, and fun. God revealed His purpose and has shown His meaning through the world He made. In the same way, creation of the planet without the formation of man would be meaningless.

Motion and purpose were established in the formation of man. The world was no longer dormant. There was immediate movement. Mankind could not live without God's desires or permission in their lives. God's personality and likeness could not be known without the creation of man. It was in the image of man that God's image and nature is known. Man is the purposed meaning of the creation. Man is the desire of the creator. God. "…created all things, and by your will (and purpose) they exist and were created" Revelation 4:11.

To make the life of man better and more meaningful, He created woman. Woman became the focus and added purpose for man's life. Creation without woman removed purpose of continuing posterity from his life. Without her, he became void of function. In the same way creation of the planet without the formation of man would be meaningless. God needs His own image to implement or carry out His own nature. Man's same need caused God to create woman for man. The image he needed was created to bring purpose to His life and allow the expression of his nature.

Man is the manifestation of God's nature while woman is the expression of the admirable divine nature. Woman embodied the exceptional El Shaddai attributes of God. Thus, man and woman as one in marriage complete the indescribable nature and purpose of God in a limited way.

This limitation is expressed through natural make up of man. But the limitlessness of His ability is displayed through spiritual purpose being awakened and exercised. This spiritual part became imprisoned by sin, but through Christ we have been liberated from that imprisonment. Now mankind has freedom and victory to show His purpose. The work of Jesus, in a world marred by sin, perfected the work of image repairer and image restorer for man. This was through the atoning death of Christ and his resurrection. We are no longer spiritually limited.

Woman became the glory and make-up of man—the completion of man—the finality of God's creation—and, the purposed meaning for man's existence.

Man is the purpose and meaning for creation. The first letter "M" in marriage speaks of how important this value of life is. Man finds his meaning in his wife and vice versa. The meaning of life, the joy of life, and all accomplishments of man and woman have been placed in each other. Man and woman, husband and wife find fulfillment of purpose while living their united life as one flesh.

This first letter may sound repulsive to the growing population of singles. Many are either self made, or conditionally made to live solitary lives in our society. Most singles today are taking shelter under the pretense of professionalism and/or choice. Yet they are deeply wounded and unfulfilled because God's principle (His Word) cannot be twisted by modern philosophies without the truth of God's principles. They embrace the ignorance. His Word is an eternally secured source of truth. The Bible says the Word of God cannot be broken.

If God created man and woman for a purposed balanced society, then that is how He wants it to be. Everything was created by God for the delight of Adam initially, but creation for Adam had no meaning or fulfillment without Eve's miraculous creation. Adam found his meaning in Eve; thus, everything and purpose outside her became meaningless. Exploration to gain understanding of the purpose of creation became a delightful engagement to Adam. He found the scope of meaning through the sovereign creation of his wife, Eve.

Does that mean singles cannot find their fulfillment in life? No! They can find meaning in external accomplishments for purposes for which they have programmed themselves. The purpose that gives joy brings them a form of contentment, but they certainly cannot find the true meaning of who they are—whom God has purposefully created them to be—the true meaning of life—without their completion in marriage or covenanted devotion to God.

Woman is first and foremost the true meaning of man. Man is created to search for purpose or meaning in everything. God created man with the passion for meaning. Man's life is accomplished when meaning is found within things he lives for. We all know how far man has gone in search of meaning and purpose for life. Man is created with the ability to explore research, dig out, get to the bottom, and forge ideas and find new ways of creation. This is the basic reason for new innovations, rapid growth and development. The meaning of life, man's reason to live is the creation of woman; and, the purpose of creation of woman is the creation of man. The Bible said God told the woman, that "her desire shall be to (rule over and honor him like a king) her husband, and he shall have the final decision, or rule over her" (Genesis 3:16).

This may or may not be the reason for the fall. Some understand this passage to be the result of their sin in the Garden. Besides, the original purposed intent of God was she was to respect her husband and fulfills his needs. That was the original intent. She was to complete Adam's purpose so as to fill the void and emptiness within Adam. This result was true. Whether sin occurred or not her original role has been divinely set. Man has enormous inner motivation to seek purpose and to find meaning through many things of life. The Bible said that man desperately tries to discover and search for meaning outside God. But, he cannot find it, because every creature cries to someone superior for livelihood (Ecclesiastes 8:17).

He tries with every bit of his inner energy to find purpose. Though he strives he will not be able to comprehend it all because the purpose of his being is to serve God. He's designed to discover real meaning for his existence in his wife, and together they are equipped and fashioned for fulfilling the purpose of God.

Man outside marriage does not understand himself. Even though everything around him seems to be appealing to him, his lonely life deprives him of meaning and purpose for his own existence. It is frustrating to have all your potential stuck inside without pointing at any source for that potential. The result is you are being imprisoned within yourself.

God's Purpose Drives A Marriage For A Lifetime

For life to be meaningful to man, he has need of reproducing or giving birth to himself. Woman, before she was brought forth from man, was already his worth and true meaning. She was the true identity of man, that which motivates him to be man. She enables man to reproduce himself; thereby making him find God's purpose and meaning for his dreams, goals and the purpose of life. Thank God for godly wives. No wonder the Bible says "whoever finds a wife finds a good thing (Proverbs 18:22) AND finds favor from the Lord." When we are able to find meaning in life we will have confidence to enjoy life to the maximum fulfillment.

In this world, man's focus is finding his dreams, and discovering how to achieve his life's divine purpose. We certainly know that man; woman and humans have kept busy searching for meaning and purpose in life, since the creation of the world. This will not cease until man finally returns to his pre-Adamic state—back into that Garden of God where he will ultimately find rest for his soul. But, until then, dreams still need meaning or interpretations (Genesis 40:5, 11); and historical events still need adequate cause for their creation (Deuteronomy 6:20). In the same way, troubles of life helps us to find new meanings to stabilize life style (Job 7:16; Ecclesiastes 6:4). In the same vein, our visions need correct meaning assigned to them (Daniel 2:45; 4:19; 7:19; 8:16; Acts 10:17) and parables used by our Lord Jesus Christ often need interpretations for them.

Likewise, customs, cultures, symbols, significant forms of languages of this modern generation need to be explored as to meaning and purpose (I Corinthians 14:11). Languages that are in this world today, however numerous they are, are for the purpose of enabling communication. As such, none are to be used for the sake of mere show. Those empowered to speak languages can enjoy and find meaning in them. All these are creative challenges that keep man busy searching for the meaning of words and how to best interpret the purpose for them.

The creation of man and woman makes meaning out of the rest of the creatures God created. God found meaning in Himself for creating man. On earth without the creation of man, God will not be known. Man would not exist and this world literally would be meaningless. Therefore, God made man in His own image. "In the likeness of God, He made man" (Genesis 1:27). This is God's purpose for the creative ability of man. Thus, marriage between husband and wife fosters the interpretation of the meaning of life and clarifies finding its expression in the covenant and vows made to each other. It demands fulfilling each other's divine purpose.

The marital institution is the school that interprets and purposes the true meaning of the mysterious term, "one flesh." It explains the dynamics of "bone of my bones and flesh of my flesh" and how two can become one, yet each retains unique identity. Marriage provides someone to depend upon and assurance for those who have decided to fulfill God's divine mandate, His purpose, in this world.

Man finds meaning for his life, sees his weaknesses, strengths, purpose, likes and dislikes through the mirror of his life, his wife.

It is a place where women find the joy, strength, covering, peace and fulfillment of their creation through their own mirror, image-man. Woman came out of man; men also by birth came out of woman. This great puzzle of life certainly needs purpose revealed through explanation, exploration and meaning. Thus when children are born into the union

God's Purpose Drives A Marriage For A Lifetime

they resemble their parents, extending family purpose into the future.

Husband and wife as part of parenting help their children find their true identity and purpose for existence.

Once man finds his meaning in his wife and vice versa, they both turn to the source of all life, their Creator, to find their source of life. Knowing full well that man and woman came as a result of their creator's desire to be pleased, their purposeful meaning in life brings fulfillment and rewards. The Christian family must never forget the purpose for their relationship or marriage. They are called to be together to answer the Creator's purposes. They have been called to produce divine pleasure for God's joy and meaning in this world. Further, the Christian family was created to make their creator worthy; to praise and worship their creator and to serve Him in this world. Their responsibility is to seek meaning from their Creator, thus finding purpose that easily drives their marriage and produces joy and satisfaction with life.

This institution of marriage was created to force a search for divine purpose and meaning for life.

Summary:
- Creation of man was done because God wanted us to know Him. We are a replica of Him so He would have meaning. SELAH!
- Man couldn't have known God without creation, but neither would God's nature have been known to us.
- Man without woman was void of function, without posterity, without expression.
- No matter what philosophy the world believes, only the Bible truth is eternally pure and secure.

Purpose Driven Marriage

> - Singles may find a form of completion in external purposes, still they will not experience the true meaning of life unless in marriage or a covenanted devotion to God.
> - Man searches for meaning, but outside marriage man doesn't understand himself.
> - Marriage is like a school that interprets and teaches the true meaning and purposes of "one flesh."

Questions to Focus on Chapter 4 Insight:
1. How did creation of man cause God to have meaning?
2. How did the devil and demons come to be? (Two possible explanations are possible, because the devil cannot create anything.)
3. What two things were established in the formation of man?
4. How did woman cause man to have meaning, why did God create her?
5. When Jesus was sent to atone for man, what happened to us spiritually?
6. Why did the fall happen? Was Adam not doing his duty? Was Eve a sinner or was she acting on behalf of Adam? Was it man's exploratory nature that had him out of position—allowing Eve to talk with a serpent?
7. Human search for meaning has been since the creation of the world? Will it ever cease?
8. Could we say that all creation exists for the good of mankind?
9. Who are the three partners in every marriage?
10. To whom should praise be extended for this brilliant creation purpose?

Chapter 5

Appreciation

A--stands for appreciation.

Although appreciation and passion are not the same, yet one may possibly accompany the other. Passion could manifest externally the attributes of appreciation. Passion denotes the starting of manifestation of sensitivity. Passion generates because of impressions on the senses; from the operation of reason—by which good or evil is foreseen; and from recalled memories. Thus, appreciation expresses our deepest sensitivities to inner delights. It could arise from a vision of God's goodness; a husband's actions; a wife's love and care; the children's good grades; being encouraged by a godly example at school; or, of any action that raises a flag of delight, joy, peace or expressed hope.

The Bible introduced appreciation by explaining the sensation of delight and joy at the creation of Eve. She was given as an awesome surprise to Adam. Adam was asleep when God took one of the "round things" (either a rib or cell) to create woman. In Genesis 2:23 it says, "And Adam said, this is now bone of my bones, and flesh of my flesh: she shall be called woman, because she was taken out of man." Adam saw his wife and appreciated her beauty and named her woman.

The words of Adam not only appreciated God, who could do such a miraculous thing, but appreciated what was taken out of him. He was awed! She was another unique being whom he called "Eve." This man appreciated and recognized that this beauty was a creation divinely created as a companion—for his benefit. God fashioned and provided her to satisfy his hungry heart and provide a way to fulfill his divine appointment with purpose.

Literally Woman "came from Man."

The creatures that had already passed before him were not suitable or fit for him. For this reason it was said in Genesis 2:20, "for Adam there was not found a help meet for him…" But when he saw the woman who came from him, he was stirred. He felt all the attractions which would consequently satisfy his God designed emotional, physical, and aesthetic hungers. He was made aware that his joy was in her person. He knew this new creature was suitable for companionship. At that realization, he burst out with an exuberant appreciative word, "she shall be called woman." The term for woman is *isnsna* and for-man is *isn*. "Woman" is derived from the word for "man." Literally woman came from man.

Bone of my bone also signifies that now indeed his purpose was clarified, or now, finally—at last she completed him as the right makeup. Eve was the "fit-one." She had all the qualities needed for man to have a fit help meet.

Mark 10:7-9, "for this cause (purpose) shall a man leave his father and mother, and cleave to his wife, and they twain shall be one flesh." The word "cleave" (*dahaq*) means to "give himself to" his wife (his own wife). That is why the first recognition of the emotional verbal outburst of joy was presented by man in deep appreciation for the creation of woman. You appreciate anything by your description of it as well as by your treatment of it. Words and actions are indicative of appreciation.

The Bible says in Job 12:11 "Doth not the ear try words? And the mouth tastes its meat?" The ear tries words and the mouth speaks based on what the ear hears. Words are very important. They are the channel through which the heart expresses its joys or struggles.

Job 34:3, the same word "for the ear trieth words, as the mouth tasteth meat." If it sounds right, it will cause joy and peace. If it sounds wrong, it will cause wounds, hurts and despair. Words thrown at each other are very important. They either cause healing or wounding to the other person. Husbands and wives must learn to use the Word of God to address any situation in their lives that directly results from bruising words. They are to avoid negative and destructive words that could not only prevent the presence of God in their homes, but become destructive to the purpose for their health and union. Remember, marriage partners are bone of bone and flesh of flesh. Appreciative words are to commend the other individual for their hard work, challenging work days, neat and tidy home, good meals, welcoming atmosphere, and peaceful

Purpose Driven Marriage

home coming. Most of all, we need to give thanks to God for being the planner, the supplier and sustainer of all things.

Look at what the Bible has to say about appreciating words in Proverbs 16:21, "the wise in heart shall be called prudent; and the sweetness of the lips increaseth learning."

In verse 24, of Proverbs 16 we find out that "pleasant words are like a honey comb, sweetness to the soul, and health to the bones." I want you to hear the phrase "health to the bones." Many couples, including Christian have destroyed their God-appointed partners with words of hurtful curses delivered by abusive, seemingly demonic oppressed tongues. Check to see who is using your tongue.

Words have caused internal suffering producing painful consequences in many good homes. Parents shape the purpose and destiny of their children by calling and describing their lives with all kinds of demeaning words. Children who are hearing negative words all of the time start acting them out. They internalize what they hear their parents say. Unwittingly their actions become almost exactly the words that their parent used to describe them.

Proverbs 17:27, says "He that hath knowledge spares his words: and a man of understanding is of an excellent spirit." Ecclesiastes 9:17 says "the words of wise men are heard in quiet more than the cry of him that rules among fools." These are the words of God. They teach us the basic principles of proper relationship. You can break customs and traditions. You can change times; but, God's purpose guiding principles are not to be broken because the results will be destruction and death.

God's Purpose Drives A Marriage For A Lifetime

Ecclesiastes 10:12 says "the words of wise man's (husband and wife) mouth are gracious: but the lips of a fool will swallow him up." This gives us clues to instruct husbands to use words which express appreciation of their wife's support in the home, intelligence, actions, and activities. And likewise it is wisdom for the wife to speak enriching words to her husband.

When talking about words of appreciation, the book of Song of Solomon, Chapters 2 and 4 give a visual description of how a king values his queen and describes physical details of her body. The same type response was recorded by the queen to the king. Please take your Bible and read Chapters 2 through 4 of Song of Solomon. Appreciating one another through words that are sweetly applied keeps the family strong and fosters enjoyment of lasting intimacy.

In Proverbs 12:18, "There is that speaks like the piercing of a sword but the tongue of the wise is health." Our words must be appreciative and express what we feel towards each other. Words are wise when they indicate our love and affection for each other. Affection is defined as a determined favor toward a mental place of special attention; or, warmth of mind toward a particular being or thing. It holds a middle place between disposition and passion. Our affection finds its expression through our actions.

Our appreciation for God's grace finds its expression through our affections for Him and His words. Expression is then directed to God through praise songs, worship, and exhorting His name above all names.

Affection toward God is defined as a vigorous and sensible exercise of the inclination and will of the soul towards our creator. Affections are the springs of action that fit our nature. This is so true that, without the highest perception of truths and purpose giving relationship with God, we are reduced to an inactive, unproductive state. The Bible teaches us that relationship with God is nothing if it is not accompanied by affections. Scriptures that speak about this truth are: (Deuteronomy 6:4-5; 3:6; Romans 12:11; I Corinthians 13:13; Psalms 27:14). Deuteronomy 6:4-5 exhorts us, "Hear, O Israel the LORD our God, the LORD is one!" Thus, we appreciate and express our inward affections towards each other by our words.

Our affection, however, is not based on the external ordinances. Nor is it based on attraction that exists in the external. It is based on inner spiritual qualities, built in purposes of God, of the type that result in moral excellence. It produces the effect of obedience toward God within the family unit. God's words filled with truth and life become the final attributes of expression.

Not only is appreciation expressed by positive words but also by positive acts. That is, words put into action. Appreciation is acted out toward the other person in different ways. Action sometimes speaks louder than your voice. Most often women use actions as their means of communication. Actions have become ways in which we communicate and express our feelings to one another. The power of activity is put into motion through different moods such as joy or sadness. The value of the relationship and oneness is displayed through actions. Husband and wife must be careful about doing negative actions because they usually are not helpful to their relationship.

Appreciation in action indicates that neither of you consider anything too big or too small for each other.

Husband who is appreciating his wife could sometimes cook for her, take care of the children at times, or regularly clean the house. He can do this and still be committed to his responsibility, but not confined to a responsibility. Wife in appreciation of God's blessing for her husband can go to work for the family; provide financial base for the up keep of the family; and, do whatever it takes guided by the principles of the Bible to take care of her home. These actions are done with humility, submission, and appreciation of God's grace towards her husband and her house.

Appreciation defies roles, rules, regulations and responsibilities.

Appreciation defies roles, rules, regulations and responsibilities. It is a condition of the heart. Husband and wife must come together and accept each other for who they are and where they are. Further they will necessarily appreciate the fact that both of them cannot achieve their divine purposes without the other. Their actions toward each other's and their children's needs prove their dependence and their reliance on God for perfection and achievement.

The husband recognizes the limitation he has without his wife and likewise the wife acknowledges her limitation when her husband's not involved. Yet, they both recognize their marriage to be the completion of divine purpose. Neither is required to be perfect but they must be appreciative of what God has given them. Both realize they couldn't be so intelligent and sufficient apart from each other. That was the reason for their marriage. Appreciating actions is the best medicine for healing broken families. God knows it is not best for a man to be alone. That loneliness creates a void and emptiness; thus creating the need for God to form woman whom man could fully appreciate. He created somebody like him, someone from him, and somebody for him.

Appreciation may be expressed by mental, physical or spiritual actions. Wise couples sing praises to God and to each other.

Appreciation could be expressed by financial gains, gifts or other material things. It could be mental, physical and spiritual expression. When it is expressed, without exception it should be done from the inside of the heart without expecting a pay back or making a demand. The results will produce a sacrificial and meaningful praise of value and worth of that individual.

The husband and wife will be wise to sing praises to God and to each other. They should show value of their time together by telling each other how they love and appreciate each other. Remember, couples do not show appreciation only through words but they have the option to allow their actions of appreciation speak louder than their words.

Giving ourselves to each other means we are lost to ourselves. We no longer think independently or act selfishly, but act in the interest of the other person. The husband takes care of the wife as he would take care of himself; the wife does the same for him. The couple accepts the strengths and weaknesses of their partner. Personal giftings or lack of gifts does not matter. Positions or lack of them becomes as nothing and disappears into thin air. Both of them embrace the struggles within the house. Any name calling or passing of blame—whether for competency or incompetency—become a taboo. The two loud speakers in the family—money and health—become controllable with the prayerful heart and the Holy Spirit's intervention. Greed and pride find another place to mark their destruction. We must give the Word of God total credence in the family. In olden days, husbands worked to provide for the needs of the family. But today, usually both of them must work to provide for the family. Christian couples find it necessary to create time to be with one another, the children, giving space for stability and healthy growth.

What you don't give time to, you can't understand. Time is expensive.

What you don't give time to, you can't understand. Time has become an expensive commodity—one that cannot be priced. Giving time to know each other, help each other and care for the children will save a lot of marriages from crashing prematurely. Husband and wife should give attention to their children before the children develop their own patterns for problem solving. There are

Purpose Driven Marriage

times of intervention in children's lives that are crucial to the development of the children. Once the parents miss the opportune time, it's always too late to recover the loss. As a result of this critical timing parents must learn to give consistent attention to the upbringing and rearing of their children. I don't mean mothers only—unless you are a single parent—but both mothers and fathers. In a divorced home, Biblical purpose that supports the principle of love and fear of God will really help.

This is the Biblical idea of giving yourselves totally to each other. The purposed result will be stimulation and growth of a healthy relationship. These suggestions are ways to give genuine active expression of appreciation to each other. It is most effectively demonstrated through actions, rather than words.

Summary:
- Appreciation and Passion are related in that they grow together based on different impressions of the senses, reason and various good experiences.
- Woman literally came from man and Adam was delighted, naming Eve woman. Literally "out of man."
- Adam appreciated Eve by his declaration of his inner delight with her, calling her woman and cleaving to her as his own "flesh of my flesh, and bone of my bone."
- Words are tried by our ears. It is important to use the Word of God when hurtful things have been said to you by a spouse. They can bruise and wound the mate!
- Uplifting and heartfelt compliments will build a home and the wise are of few words, full of grace and support.

- Affection is based upon internal spiritual qualities; women usually demonstrate affection in their actions toward the person for whom they have affection. An affectionate man may sometimes cook a meal for his wife defying man's typical role.
- Appreciating actions often mend broken families, showing affection is present.

Questions to Focus on Chapter 5 Insight:
1. Why did Adam call Eve woman, not Eve?
2. Positive words will prevent hurt in the home. Why is this true? Give examples.
3. Do parental words even limit a child's character and accomplishments? How?
4. How did the king talk to the queen? Is that appropriate?
5. Giving ourselves means we are lost to self and ready to give to the relationship. Our time given means we value the relationship more than anything. Are you willing to do this to help fix any hurts?

Chapter 6
Respect

The letter "R" in Marriage represents respect.

Respect in the home is a medium of meaningful communication between husband and wife. It creates an awesome atmosphere of friendliness and accommodation. Marriage is a school where respect as the proper meaningful and purposeful language is expressed to its fullest extent. If this simple description of respect is true, then successful marriages need to pay special attention to this expression.

If respect is lost there will be nothing to preserve the home as a lasting purpose driven relationship.

God's Purpose Drives A Marriage For A Lifetime

Christian families have been taught through ages that communication with God is life's first priority, its purpose. It flows freely from our respect for God. Our respect for God results in accepting and loving Him. Out of respect to God develops trust, obedience and service. Our respect to Him allows Him to communicate and make Himself accessible to us. If respect is lost there will be nothing to preserve the home as a lasting purpose driven relationship. Thus any loss of this essential key, respect, from the family must be regained. Respecting yourself in the home will carry over to how you treat yourself outside the house. I define respect as an attitude of reverence and appreciation for the differences of values and significance toward the person or thing that is esteemed.

Respect is esteemed value or importance given openly to another person in the family circle. It is the expression of appreciative differences admired and revered in the other individual as a divinely purposed unique husband, wife or child. This in turn is compounding the expression of God's purposeful agenda in creating mankind in His image.

The character, natures, attributes, likes and dislikes of each individual are unique. As such they ought to be respected and treated as an image reflecting the same God who brought the couple together (Genesis 9:5-6). In the Christian home, a healthy marriage enjoys God's conscious natural respect.

Respect is not given out of obligation. Many people have misunderstood the Biblical duties of women to men based on Ephesians 5:22, which states, "Wives, submit yourselves unto your husbands, as unto the Lord." In the context of the entire text the referenced passage explains the fact that husbands were heads of the house, as Christ is the head of the church. Thus, the passage is not saying that respect for the husband should be seen as obligatory, but that which comes out of the nature and heart of the woman.

Obligatory respect results in intimidation, fear, enslavement, or a bossy male attitude.

God's image and creation design in the woman makes her naturally want to respect her husband regardless of any circumstances. Obligatory respect results in intimidation, fear, enslavement, or a bossy male attitude. Often it ends in resentment, argument, and communication deficiency which, if it is out of control or mismanaged, mostly ends in divorce.

Most domestic violence could be avoided by extending respect toward the other spouse's feelings, desires and need for fulfillment.

Most violence occurs between husbands and wives because demands are made on each other without respecting each other's feelings, desire, fulfillments, etc.

God's Purpose Drives A Marriage For A Lifetime

Everything God fashioned was created with respect to bring out the exact creation purpose. Respect motivated manifestation in creation. To respect God is to allow Him to manifest His glory in our lives. To disrespect Him is to bring His wrath upon ourselves. God created marriage as an institution in which He could manifest His divine purposes. In this world, respect for one another makes God's intentions and purpose come to fruition within the home. Respect also means: to be tolerant of each other's strengths and weaknesses; to have a broad or open mind toward each other's creative ability; and, that the earthy manifestation of divine fulfillment is when each honors the other.

According to the Bible women are gifted so that they naturally respect through the grace of God and are able to oversee their husbands and homes showing respect (Ephesians 5:33). The children are to respect their parents being obedient to them; as the woman is encouraged to respect her husband insuring their lasting relationship. Virtuous, Biblical women characters were respectful of their husbands. They showed this in their words (the way they talked to or about him), behavior, actions, and attitude.

In the Biblical days, godly women used the term "lord" out of respect, instead of their husband's name. In my culture, the husband's body posture is used in greeting. Body language is used in communicating to each other. Preferences were given to the husband in most decision making. Respectful words were used when addressing their husbands; and, in New Testament times they covered their heads in the religious services and as expressions of respect to their husband. I Corinthians 11:7 provides a key. "The woman is the glory of man." Their attitudes were of submissive reverence to God's prescribed order.

Purpose Driven Marriage

This godly respect in the home today has been mistakenly viewed as enslavement, depravity and beneath woman's dignity by women. The modern disease of woman's liberation philosophy or women's rights activists has viewed the humbling Biblical language of family dignity as a taboo. This group has treated the secrete things of God and the temple of God with total disrespect and perverseness. They term it "Women's Liberation." The group degrades the husband-father's position and tramples on the holy and sacred things of God. This same sick attitude is trying to act as a stereotype and creep in as a common trademark for a Christian's home. This explains one reason why the divorce rate is outrageously high within the Christian community.

As a godly wife, your respect for your husband will give you more of his attention. It will deflate his egoistical bullying attitude and calm his outbursts of raging anger. This will free him from these things which are not part of God's purpose in the lives of a genuine born again Christian. Biblically, a wife is gifted with a respectful nature by God. Your respect for your husband is not to be based upon how he treats you, loves you, or cares for you. Respect will be flowing from your divine nature (God's purpose) toward your husband. Respect for your mate will be given seriously with humility. There will be a lack of any proud talk or actions (2 King 1:14, 3:14, Esther 1:20, Proverbs 11:6).

Women, if you want to maintain your homes in peace, please take time to review <u>Marriage Not Manage Tools for a Successful Marriage's</u>[1] chapters on effective communication at home. The key ideas include: respecting your husband—not out of obligation, not because you are

---

[1]. P. Obadare, <u>Marriage Not Manage</u>…, London, Wisdom Network Charities, 2008, pp.59-65. Order: www.AuthorHouse.com ISBN 97-814389238-26.

God's Purpose Drives A Marriage For A Lifetime

intimidated or commanded—but as a reflection of the nature of God in you. The tools must be used with reverence toward God first and then to make your family God's home.

The husband's role is respecting his wife by loving her: The same Ephesians 5:25 says "Husband love your wife, even as Christ also loved the church, and gave himself for it." Christian husbands should determine to demonstrate Biblical immeasurable love towards their wives. That demonstrated love is respect; and, what we don't love we cannot truly respect. It is out of your respect for your wife that you can love her unconditionally.

The love Jesus extended to us was unconditional. That same magnitude of agape' love was the same pattern of love He desires us to show toward our wives. This means you may find it hard to relate to her nagging attitude, her pride, her provocative verbiage, her explosive anger, or her aggressive jealousy. Regardless of all these, your love for her must still allow you to show respect to her by your treatment and handling of her (I Peter 3:7).

<u>Respect for your wife may be shown by:</u>

Gently expressing disagreements
Pleasantly handling frustrations in love and care towards her (This will ease any tensions in the house.)
You refuse to discourage her beneficial activities in or out of the home
You avoid speaking harshly, arrogantly or showing your masculine strength against her
When she argues and strongly disagrees with your views, you take the nature of God as the Father and husband (Also, do not double check to be certain you are holding the Lord's response. She is your help meet.)

Providing help and guidance in the care of the home as she directs, though the wife may be deceived and Biblically she is called a weaker partner (I Peter 3:7)
Respect is accorded for her advice
Nuptial rights and privileges to your wife are accorded as if it were to your own body
A godly example is demonstrated in your community (I Thessalonians 4:12)
Help her at home, cooking for her, drawing her bath water—washing her back, cleaning the home, doing laundry, baby sitting, and doing anything that makes her happy.

This is love; this is what God calls family. He designed it to fulfill His ordained purpose. This type of respect is not demanded or obligatory toward your wife. You extend it because it is your God given nature to love and respect her as God loves His own children. That's why you do it. The husband, as the head of the home, sets the tone so the wife and children respond with all honor and unquestionable regard toward the respectful, Godly husband.

Respect is the key to a meaningful relationship. If a family wants to achieve the divine purpose of such a union, respect must be given adequate attention. The society or community of today would be wise to go back to the example of the old family unit, and examine the keys to their longevity.

- Respect for each other that dignifies their marriages is shown.
- Respect for one another's cultures, in case of cross-culture marriages will be given.
- Respect for one another's emotional needs in terms of individual desire for God will be found coupled with respect for physical need in terms of sexual relationship. This

important facet of respect should be taken seriously as sacred and fulfilling. Genesis 1:25 says Adam and Eve were: Naked and not ashamed.

Acting on all these should help to stimulate Godly love within marriages. Let's purpose to act with respect like we did before we got married. That was when we respected each other's ideas, customs, desires and beliefs. If we could act that way before we said "Yes, I do." we can continue the same way after we have accepted one another as one flesh (Genesis 1:24; Ephesians 5:31).

The Bible speaks of respect in many areas. Nature commands its own respect. Human government is to be respected. Human leaders are to be respected. Children are to respect their parents, and conversely, they are to be respected by their parents. God's creation and environment ought to be respected; but, when any one of these is disrespected there is chaos, anarchy, disorder, violence and destruction.

The first commandment calls us to love and obey (respect and honor) the Lord our God. Exodus 20:7

The first commandment is to respect and give honor to God's Name (Exodus 20:7; Psalms 29:2; Deuteronomy 5:11; and many others). Respect establishes a relationship with

God; the first thing is to purpose to respect His Name and His Personality.

Respect is Commanded in the Bible

The created beings of the world are to respect God. For examples: respect His presence (Exodus 3:5-6); respect His sanctuary (Leviticus 19:20; Ecclesiastes 5:1-2); respect human beings who are made in the image of God (Genesis 9:5-6; James 3:9-10); respect is commanded in marriage (Ephesians 5:21-25; Colossians 3:18-19; I Peter 3:6-7); respect our leaders (Deuteronomy 1:13-15; Proverbs 31:23; Romans 13:1-7); and respect our environment including the earth's natural resources and animals (Exodus 23:10-11; Leviticus 25:1-; Deuteronomy 22:4; 6-7; Proverbs 12:11).

What Respect is

Respect—It is acceptance of individual rights, strengths or weaknesses without dominating attempts to fix the other. It is an individual freedom without being beaten or coerced, told to shape up, or forced to fit into the acceptable pattern of the other partner. Respect is reciprocal in Biblical perspective. It instigates the love flow between the mates. So, each empowers the other to function in good health. In short, without respect, communication within relationship shuts down.

Respect in relationship also mean energy between marriage partners. It facilitates emotional attachments that allow dealing with criticism or condemnation from their partner.

Respect in relationship means gaining an understanding of individual personalities and according willingness to allow natural blending—with changes, for a healthy relationship.

In short, without respect, communication within relationship shuts down.

Respect enables truthful expression of guilt. Respect involves surrendering of an individual's sovereignty to attain a workable adjustment though there are different ethnic communities.

Respect is prioritizing each other's opinions, operations and affections. Respect gives the immediate family a priority above other families.

Respect is treating the other partner either domestically, or externally exactly the same way the other desires to be treated.

Respect says what is good for me is good for her. What is good for the husband is good for the wife. One is not above the other in giving or receiving respect.

In the subjective tone, Biblical women are to respect their husband while men were to love their wives unconditionally.

Purpose Driven Marriage

Unconditional means whether or not the husband is respected, he must still love his wife. This is a hard thing, but the same goes for the wife. She is to show respect regardless of the husband's treatment of her. It is a tough love. **But when it becomes chronic or insanely abusive, it is another situation with another solution. Jesus loves us unconditionally.**

Healthy relationship is maintained by showing ample respect for each other in order to function driven by God's purpose for a lifetime. Respectful ways of addressing each other at home before the children, parents or extended family members are necessary. Respect is shown in how each addresses the other even in their absence. In other words, respectful reference should be accorded before colleagues, at work, friends, and strangers. The old saying, "as you make your bed, so you will lay on it" is applicable.

Jokes about a spouse are always in poor taste and could lead to disrespect and other problems.

The best way to avoid trouble is to not make any jokes or derogatory comments about your spouse in any form or shape; whether it is a good or bad joke—don't make them. It could lead to disrespect for your partner. Later it could endanger the relationship. Infidelity and unnecessary flirtations or affairs may begin with negative comments about the other partner.

Pressure begins to mount up on the person based on the casual comments made about the spouse. This may not be deliberate, but because of careless talk and comments, issues begin to develop from various areas. Before the person knows it, they are in deep trouble. Any healthy relationship will avoid this type of talk and keep this destructive fire from burning. Notice, this difficulty started from disrespectful comments about their mate to other people in the presence or in the absence of their mate. Many of these compromises have escalated ending in divorce, separation, or loss of life.

Respect is important in relationship and it builds a by-lateral structure within a home instead of a dictatorship.

Respect is a recovering agent. It allows recovery of a person from emotional damages. It repositions trust. It opens sealed communication doors and shuts doors of speculation. When this important tool no longer operates in a meaningful relationship either in a Christian or non-Christian home, the relationship falls into a deep coma usually resulting in death or amputation.

Respect creates a by-lateral relationship. This relationship is based on mutual agreement and partnership rather hierarchical institution. The husband opts to help the wife in the kitchen regardless of his institutional title. When he comes to clean, cook, care for children, and take clothes to laundry, both mates realize that they both worked outside the home and both need to work in the home. No one thinks the domestic work is the other's job, nor are they sitting in the living room, chatting with friends, watching television, playing games, busy talking on phone, or waiting for the other person to double work, taking take care of the busy body partner. (In this case, it could be man or woman; but, I know the buck usually falls on the man's side.)

The woman rightfully becomes irritated when her man comes home and does not participate in anything. She receives no help, not even with the children's homework. Most women don't complain because they know how to pay back—they get even! Another may complain and make it known that they don't appreciate it; nevertheless, men are not that sensitive to this type of emotional outcry of feelings. While the woman is doing her second full time job, the man is gathering his energies together for the night. He's saving—or gathering strength—for a romantic moment. During this time the woman is working as hard as he is resting, spending all her remaining energy to prepare for the next day. Bed time comes. The woman is worn out and tired, while the man is refreshed and ready for romance. He's not aware, but at this time is when the woman settles down and begins to reflect on the activities of the day. She's begun to make the mental shift to the next day.

No help + No respect = No romance tonight!

Romantic time for the woman is a reflective moment. She begins remembering past daily activities, recalling statements, actions, and the responses of her husband during the time when she wanted help. The woman pounders on the respect accorded her during the past day, or on the neglect she received both at work, school, and home. Her energy and hormones shut down. Her body language states flatly "I am not in the mood."

Now the husband who is ready to release his stored energy soon finds out that, the doors are shut to his avenue for intimacy. He feels like a sports car with the engine revving and with a flat tire. Regardless of how powerful the engine, he cannot move with a flat tire—unless he's dragging the rim ruining the tire. Anyway, it can only be dragged for a short distance. The woman is spent, worn out, and flat on her back ready to sleep. Here she faces the need of her man, one that also has to be met—in whatever way. Some woman would just give in to the man to go ahead and do what he needs to enjoy himself. They are not emotionally a participant and their body is just being dragged along to accommodate the moment.

Eventually, if this continues it will damage the personality of the woman. She will continue to change and become a total "careless" person who says, "I am used to it." Or, "I can't be bothered" just to maintain peace. Some women are brave enough to face the consequences and will refuse to be used or to give in to the whims of their husband.

A man who will want to enjoy a romantic, pleasurable night with his wife should have been responsible enough to work alongside his wife helping do their chores so that they shared the work equally and she was relieved of some pressure during the evening. Again, as the old saying illustrates," you lay in your bed in the evening the way you made it in the morning." Or as others would say, "You make your bed hard—you'll sleep on it."

Respect and real enjoyment is a contribution from both mates to making things work together. Women don't want to feel like a remote control that a man presses to get her to begin responding. Wives take time to emotionally think through processes—even intimacy.

Some men are so strongly addicted to "their" games or sports that they choose to satisfy their interest at the expense of a meaningful time with their wives. Because of the man's emphasis, the women come to believe the best time to get a man to slow down, talk, or reason through is when he is amorous, the "time of man." This should not be! This is not the method or time to communicate sensible things to a man. Ideally, it should be a time of consummation of enjoyable moments of shared activities that have taken place during their day.

Relationships which are based on compulsion and demanded rights, not on respect and consideration, cause damage to the family and end up producing a chaotic home.

Respect is the purpose power source that vitalizes lifelong marriages.

Summary:
- ➢ If respect is lost there will be no school in the marriage to teach meaningful and purposeful language in the home.
- ➢ Communication flows naturally out of respect, and that flow leads to accepting and loving God as well as our marriage partner.
- ➢ Respect is giving esteem and importance opening to another person in the family circle
- ➢ Respect may be shown in many different ways. Review the list of suggestions.

God's Purpose Drives A Marriage For A Lifetime

- Being tolerant of each other's strength and weaknesses shows respect.
- God intended the husband father be respected. Trendy living sometimes removed the respect thereby weakening marriage among Christians. Respect strengthens women and men in their marriages and living out creation purposes.
- Husbands are commanded to love their wives. Wives are told to respect their husbands. Agape love was gifted to all believers and needs to be applied lavishly in marriage and at home.
- Respect is a key that unlocks many good things in marriage. Learning to give respect is as valuable as giving time to your mate.
- Intimacy is an outgrowth of the respect given to the mate prior to approaching the romantic activities. Women and men differ in their approach to sexual intimacy and each mate needs to develop tolerance for the others needs.

Questions to Focus on Chapter 6 Insight:
1. Do you ever say, "I can't get any respect around here!" What's wrong and how can you fix it—quickly?
2. Does respect ever come from obligation?
3. Let's say a wife is afraid to speak about her feelings to her husband. What may be happening in the home—behind closed doors?
4. What word sequences cause you to react with upset, anger or near anger?
5. Do you use body language or speak to your mate first after coming home and entering a room where your mate is waiting? If not, why not? That's an easy way to say I respect you and you are important to me?

6. In showing the glory of man how do you think a woman should act toward her own husband?
7. What are some of the benefits of showing respect in marriage?

Chapter 7

Responsibility

The other letter "R" means Responsibility.

Marriage is a great responsibility. It is an institution that is to be built. The union of the husband and wife is the purpose for the foundation upon which the marriage (building) is designed to be established.

Husband and wife begin to gather together tools and explore avenues for crafting the structure of this building. In fact, the first thing both of them should secure is faith in the Chief Corner Stone on which the pillar of the building is to be rested. The pillar is none other than Jesus the Christ, the Savior, and the Messiah. Once this corner stone is in place, the foundation purpose rests securely.

The second important thing necessary for the proper building of this marriage (building) is the architectural drawing. The plan for the building, all the drawings and explanations, are in the Word of God. The road map leads to building strong homes. The Word of God directs the husband and wife as the builders of their building. The Word directs as to where to put what, and how to prioritize the important aspects of this building. The Holy Bible contains the blue print for building a solid home.

After the plan they need the energy, the encouragement, and the wisdom to keep the marriage building usable. At this time, they need the Holy Spirit to help them manage the marriage and to become responsible in God's grace. Responsibilities consist of taking charge of what has been committed into one's hand. It also requires doing the tasks as it has been patterned and purposed by the one who committed it to the marriage partners. They must be fully aware of their accountability to God since He is the one who allowed married couples such privileges.

Responsibility calls for accountability. Responsibility is being in charge of something which makes one work hard because someone is giving oversight. He or she must give account to authority. Therefore, as an example, an architect is required to draw plans to fulfill the obligation, wisdom, skill, energy, patience, faith, gifts or whatever other attributes would be required for getting the job done. He is responsible for his part of the building. Jesus spoke about a nobleman who called his servants and delivered to them talents and instructed them to occupy until he came back (Luke 19:13). Thus, the family is equipped with every tool to become profitable to God. Husband and wife have been given the purpose mandate to occupy the home, to work, and to become productive for someone. We are to use all spiritual resources and the freedom of time God has assigned us to make the family work. The reason God has gifted us with spiritual resources and time is because with this enormous responsibility comes enormous accountability.

God's Purpose Drives A Marriage For A Lifetime

HUSBAND'S ROLE AND PURPOSES IN MARRIAGE

Thank God we have the blue print, the Word of God. The Word of God defines our purpose and makes it easy. It gives the role and responsibilities for each marriage partner. According to the blue print, clearly woman came out of the other—out of man (Genesis 2:22-23: I Corinthians 11:8, 9, 11-12).

The duties given to man are involved with his responsibility to care for his wife--especially within the home.
(a) Protector (Matthew 1:18-24; 2:18, 19-20) or covering her (I Corinthians 11:3; Ruth 2:14-16; 3:3-15; Esther 5:1-3)
(b) Provider--work and industrious (Genesis 2:15; 3:19, 23; I Samuel 1:4-5; Exodus 21:10); food, clothing, sex, and pleasure Genesis 29:20 says Jacob served seven years to marry his wife Rachel.
(c) Progenitor--Leave and cleave (Genesis 2:24; Matthew 19:5; Mark 10:7-8; Ephesians 5:31).
(d) Lover— (Ephesians 5:25; Deuteronomy 24:5; Proverbs 5:18; Ecclesiastes 9:9; Ephesians 5:28-33; Colossians 3:19; I Peter 3:7). To fulfill marital duties—relating to intimacy (I Corinthians 7:3-5; Exodus 21:10-11); to be faithful to the wife (Exodus 20:14; Deuteronomy 5:18: 22:22: Malachi 2:14; Matthew 5:27-28); to praise his wife and encourage her (Proverbs 31:28). This love extended is a vital part of husbanding the wife and growing her into the fullness of God's purpose for her life. He senses just what will encourage her and cause her to work diligently toward success in skills, like writing, sewing, computer, secretarial or other areas according to her talents. He is guided by God to water and enrich her just like a gardener tends a tender flowering or fruit bearing plant. The husband is to the wife as Christ is to the church. We are subject to Christ

and He gave himself for the church. What love husbands are capable of applying to their wife! Christ's example is far beyond rough shod control of a wife. (Ephesians 5:23-27)

A husband is to follow Christ's example and love his wife as Christ loved the church and gave himself for her. (Ephesians5:25 AMP paraphrased)

The duty of the husband is to leave his family and cleave to his wife. He must leave his immediate family who could influence him or control him in his new relationship with his wife. He is to leave friends and counterparts who were his former advisers. Further, he is to leave other women friends, girl friends and any other circle of people that used to engage him. He is to leave the circle of oneness (singleness) to become whole in marriage. In leaving and cleaving to his wife, who is the other part of him, he will complete his divine nature. One helps the other to fulfill the divine purpose of God for their life time. Examine the Triune God, one God with three distinct roles and functions, yet He is one. This is the mystery: one submitting to the other for the accomplishment of the intended divine purpose. This is revelation in marriage: One becomes three.

Another unique duty or responsibility of the husband to his wife is to love her. Rather than acting as if the wife must deserve to be loved, it is the responsibility of the husband to love his wife—no matter what! It is his unique role to love her sincerely, genuinely, and unconditionally. Just as the father loves the children regardless of their behaviors, Jesus loves the Church regardless of her weaknesses. God loved the world enough to send His only begotten Son to voluntarily die for the Church. The love was not deserved. The love was even rejected; but, He was a true lover that welcomed acceptance or rejection. This type of love was demanded by the scripture from the husbands to their wives. It was love not as a result of anything, but as a divine responsibility of the husband to his wife. He is to give continuous account to God on how this responsibility is being administered in his home.

Husbands are the heads of their household. This is a responsibility which means they are to protect and act as the covering over their wives. The husband's duty is to make sure that the wife and home are secure and safe. He is to provide a safe environment for his family. He is not to expose them to unnecessary risks, temptations or dangers. His role is to take proper care of the wife. As the head, he is to give instructions, guidance and vision for the smooth running of the home. He is to look out for his wife and children defending against lies and deceptions of the enemy. He is to shield his family from ungodly influences and worldly passion. At any moment he will raise an alarm when he sees danger coming. This is the responsibility of a Godly husband to protect his Godly home.

Another important responsibility of husbands is to provide for the family. The primary role of the husband is to provide adequately for his family. Though his adequate provision is the ideal, husbands and wives often work cooperatively to provide for their homes. This seems to have happened because of changes caused by humanity's sin. The husband's provision should be furnished regardless of the wife's income or financial support. You will find this when you read the three-judiciary responsibilities of man to his wife in Exodus 21:10. He is to provide three important satisfactions for his wife. They are: security, provision, and love coupled with sexual fulfillment.

Roles have changed over the years, but the Bible truths haven't.

We know roles have changed over the years. Family values changed and affected the basic foundation of families. Families today are in trouble and deep confusion, but the Biblical foundation of man's responsibilities to their wives has not changed and will not change. We need to go back to the basic foundation, so that our families can function better. The woman as the helpmate is to be a secondary and additional means to the primary responsibility given to man as a provider for his home. And the more duties include his sexual fulfillments and responsibilities to his wife. The wife ideally does not need to solicit or demand for her rights. It is his right and his duty to perform.

Part of his responsibility is to be faithful to his wife. He's to assure the trust of his wife; to be honest; and, not hide anything from the wife. He's to be totally faithful in dealing with her emotional, mental, and spiritual needs. Many husbands think and act wrongly in assuming that, their wives have to earn their trust. The woman should not need to work to earn the trust of her husband. It is the responsibility of the husband to be and be known as being faithful to his wife. In this circumstance the idea of jealousy, which is the first indication of lack of trust, would not be allowed to harm their relationship. Although, jealousy might be a wonderful tool to maintain healthy relationships—if it is used positively and scripturally—yet its misuse could be very damaging. This important relational gift will be discussed in full detail at another time.

Another, but not the least, of man's responsibility is to praise his wife. He is to speak kind words to her, sing to her, use any and everything possible to praise her. Praise means giving honor to someone. Appreciating who a person is and what the person has done is praise. It is the duty of the husband to praise his wife using moral, financial, spiritual principles, every means to thank her for accepting him, and for putting up with him. As he praises her willingness to make the best of him, so she may accord praise to him for his valuable qualities. It is a duty not a privilege.

This concludes valuable basic responsibilities of a man to his wife from the scriptures. Again, what society says does not and cannot change what God has written. If we want to have a genuine Godly purpose for marriage, we ought to follow the plan the creator designed for man and woman.

Woman's Role and Purpose in Marriage

Woman has a rather unique role to play in making their marriage a success. The responsibilities assigned to women have been taken out of context. This causes a role reversal producing failures in family. The twisted result is replacing the original role assigned to women. Let us examine the Biblical responsibilities of women. These are not optional, but compulsory to the fulfillment of the God given role for a wife within her home.

__Woman's role in marriage success has been incorrectly viewed. In reality it is a unique and vital role in marital happiness.__

Firstly, the wives are helpers and companions to their husbands (Genesis 2:18-22). They are required to join the vision, give a supporting hand to their husbands' dreams and aspirations for their family. Their helping hands may require: work to support their husbands; fill any emotional emptiness; or, quiet their husband's anxiety. Wives are to be seen as dependable and undergirding by their husbands.

God's Purpose Drives A Marriage For A Lifetime

The role of the wife is to be (willingly helpful in assisting) submissive to and respectful toward her husband. Submission is willingly yielding energy to another person without a sense of obligation. Submission is not enslavement to the whims of her husband. It is an attribute of cheerfully accorded decisive obedience to the husband. Again, the Bible says **each should submit** to the other.

Seen this way, submission is not a weakness in women but is strength to them. It is the responsibility of a wife to submit to her husband. Thus, the husband does not have to ask for it or merit it; it is not based on the husband's love or hate. It is the duty of the wife to submit in everything to her husband. It is yielding the wife's mind, will, power, and saying to her husband: "This is done as unto God."

He is the one to whom the wife will ultimately give account. Let's see it in the light of the following scriptures (Colossians 3:18; Ephesians 3:22-24, 33; I Peter 3:1-6). In light of these scriptures, submission and respect is to be afforded to the husband without excuses. He is to be respected as the head of the house, as the governor, and as the judge of the home.

Respect should be clothed by your words, even in the way you address your husband. Disrespectful titles or names, arrogant behaviors, insult casting, and rude actions are out of line with his place in the home. Respect must be shown in posture of greetings and addressing either in private or especially in public. If the woman of today can learn the Biblical role of submission, their families will be secure and their children will be protected.

In this case, the husband should never take advantage of his wife's generous submission to him by abusing his wife. Rather, because you, as her husband you have the duty

Purpose Driven Marriage

of being her custodian. Remember, someone gave her to you--and He's God!

The responsibility of the wife is to care for her husband. Care means, tending to him, his needs, his troubles, his struggles, his frustrations, and his goals according to the guidelines of holiness and righteousness (Titus 2:4-5).

The wife is to be faithful to her husband. The husband does not have to ask for this or demand it. It is the responsibility of the wife to be faithful and trustworthy to her husband.

She is not to hold grudges, express unnecessary jealousy, or defensiveness. She is to be faithful to her husband in everything (Exodus 20:14; Deuteronomy 5:18; Numbers 5:11-31; Proverbs 23:27; Matthew 14:3-4). Faithfulness means truthfulness, holiness, purity and openness. These are measurable factors of faithfulness. She must display or demonstrate these if she is to be a woman who desires to keep her home and husband safe.

One of the energetic responsibilities of a wife is to give good counsel-advice to her husband. Wives are good counselors. This is their makeup. They are to give Godly advice to their husbands on any given situation when requested by the husband. Even when the husband did not request it; they might tactfully offer good advice to them. As helpmeet, this is part of their responsibility (Matthew 27:19; Joel 13:22; Daniel 5:10-12).

The most important role of the wife to the husband is to respect him unconditionally. Once both have agreed to marry regardless of the shortcomings of each other—the tallness, shortness, and deformities in physical or in behaviors—all these are no longer factors for comparison.

God's Purpose Drives A Marriage For A Lifetime

You are married to all the strengths and weaknesses in each other. As a result we must learn to adapt to each other respectfully. Wives are to love their husbands without comparison and without condition (Titus 2:4).

Other unique duties or responsibilities of the wife at home are: to demonstrate a goodly and Godly character; to be a positive role model in her activities; to provide support to her husband; but, also to support other families around her. She makes her family accessible to others while providing a great example of a Godly home. She pleases her husband in her community activities. Her character toward her husband attracts all his love and compassion. He is so taken with her that he is lost in her.

The responsibility of a Godly wife is as an administrator. She is to protect her home by administering the domestic and financial operations of her home. Thank God for Godly women who properly manage their husband's home and income. Over time, some men have taken over the financial things and often stresses develop if he is too stringent.

Domestically, wives work hard, cook, wash, clean, bath, nurse, manage and keep their homes in order. Godly husbands trust their wives to keep their money and administer it to the benefit of the family. Should she not be able to manage some area, she will need to exercise her wisdom and work this out with her husband.

She is an encourager, influencer and comforter to her husband. What a unique role! Fruitfulness flows from the husband—wife intimacy, for she is pleased that that part of her domestic responsibility is child bearing. She delights in being productive in her husband's home. After giving birth to children, she trains and nurtures them in the way of the Lord. Her husband gives full support and love (I Timothy 2:14-15). This is the most beautiful and pleasurable emotional duty a woman has in her home.

As maker of the home her personality determines the warmness that greets her husband when he returns home. Also, her good taste amply furnishes and makes the home warm and inviting—like she is.

These are some of the divine roles the wife is designed to play in the marriage home. However, all these responsibilities, both the husband's and wife's are based on a Godly foundation. Neither of them should see their role as superior or inferior, but as a responsibility assigned to them by God's purpose. They are to be fruitful, multiply and prepare to give account to the creator on the last day.

Responsibility of the family unit lies with both husband and wife who are by-laterally responsible to each other and then both to God's purpose.

The first responsibility is becoming educated so we know what ought to be done and how to add value to each other. So it is not only in a family setting, but in every group involvement. Of late it has become increasingly more difficult for a person to know what is or what is not required, to enable proper functioning.

Responsibility could be self assigned, or assigned by another. Regardless of the assignee, the fact remain, there is a role one has to play in fulfilling any responsibility which in turn calls for accountability.

It is man's place to stand for his family. He must be responsible to deal with any fault, and if there is problem in the home he must not pass off the blame to any other family member.

The wife's role must allow the man to fill his responsibilities as husband of the house. The man is accountable for and to the whole family. One of the major roles of the husband is taking risks for the family especially in major decision making.

One of the major roles of the husband is taking risks for the family especially in major decision making.

The wife must trust her husband enough to allow him to make certain decisions for the family. This is part of his headship, and even if he sometimes makes a mistake, that is part of his growing enabling maturity. If she allows him to face the consequence of his decision for the family, she is acting wisely.

The husband should be prepared to be challenged, criticized and appreciated by the member of his family. If he is wise he will allow members of the family to give him feedback, either negatively or positively. Harsh words or reprisals will stop feedback!

Most times in the family, husband and wife roles are poorly defined, not written out in black and white; nor are they written in gold plate. It mostly assumes and forms a pattern of the accumulated acts throughout their entire relationship. Whatever forms is what is played out within the home.

Most families based their responsibilities and roles on oral traditions. Some are based on societal, communal or ethnical backgrounds. Most relationships are patterned after the examples seen in day to day life in their parents' home.
The result is we pattern our families after the ones we live with. On the other side of the coin, the pattern could be good or bad.

Some couples look at each other's responsibilities according the Biblical specifications; which, while it may not be written on stone it is accepted, adopted, and has been practiced for many decades. The bitter truth is that, the one who is responsible may make choices that result in the other's good or cause them misery.

In some relationships, there are role reversals some may be related to neglected responsibilities. This causes the other to assume the mate's responsibility. Roles, then responsibilities are reversed. Many of these muddled relationships end in chaotic home problems and shattered families.

There are single fathers today who have assumed the role of mothers in addition to their own role. In other single families mothers experience this doubling. Both are abnormal role reversals. The result of role reversal has caused motherless, fatherless, orphaned children, and children who have grown up in discomfort and distressed conditions.

The problem in the garden wasn't the apple in the tree, but the pair (pear) on the ground. (Dr. Grady Etheridge's Witt in memory, July 26, 1923 to May 31, 2009)

This neglect of responsibilities has a Biblical undertone. This was the circumstance in the case of Eve speaking to the serpent in behalf of her husband. She should not have entertained any conversation with the snake at all regarding the instruction God gave her husband. Adam received the instruction and it was only passed down to Eve through her husband. Even when Eve fell into that situation, the man (Adam) still had the chance of changing the atmosphere. He could have corrected the situation and reported to God seeking a remedy. The fault was Adam neglected his responsibility. Not only did he leave the woman to deal with the enemy, but he accepted her offer to join his wife in disobedient action—in spite of what the Lord told him.

He compromised God's orders and fellowship of the Creator for the pleasure of his wife's presence and participated in acting out her conviction. Once the head of the family loses the purpose of the vision, everyone else goes down with him.

The idea held in this story is that, Eve should have yielded the choice to her husband, instead of taking on this out-of-her-league task. Her decision not only broke fellowship for her and her husband, but their children who populated the world around them. This calamity shows the dire effects that neglect of responsibilities can cause. Even passing the buck may burden the other person if they are unable to carry that relayed load. She, after refraining from decision making, should have informed the devil to talk it out with her husband. Maybe he could convince her husband to eat the fruit; anyway, it was not her place or responsibility to negotiate with the devil.

The first husband, Adam was incapacitated by the love for his wife.

- He neglected his leadership role and allowed his wife to make a decision she wasn't supposed to make. This resulted in activation of the curses attached to disobedience; death in the first class, spiritual death. He must have felt that rejecting his wife's advice would not make her happy.
- He further made the mistake of listening to the one who was created for his enjoyment rather than the listening to the purposeful command of God who created and gave him the enjoyment.

It was the Adam's responsibility to protect his wife so that she wouldn't be alone with the enemy.

God's Purpose Drives A Marriage For A Lifetime

It was the Adam's responsibility to protect his wife so that she wouldn't be alone with the enemy.

Maybe it was loneliness that resulted in the devil's solicitation of Eve? The man may have been too involved in—glued to and occupied by his work, or exploring a new mineral or species.

Eve should never have been continually exposed to the rigorous persuasion of the devil. But even so, that exposure should not have been important enough to make Eve yield or Adam to sacrifice their relationship and damage their relationship with God.

The same sick thinking is affecting today's relationships—from both a woman's or man's perspective. The old serpent's tricks have not changed, and sadly, they continue working.

Factors like:
- Too much time at work
- Allowing other interests or activities to create continuous gaps
- Anxieties or stresses because of the family activities
- Love for children elevated above love for the spouse

- Extended families' injected needs, desires for service
- Time with friends
- Passion for games or sports
- Careless outings
- Self righteousness
- Compulsive Godliness; long fasts, mission outreaches, sleep deprivation
- Whatever makes one partner be alone or lonely. When long spans of time are lacking the mate's company, it creates vacuums for enemy temptations.
- One partner could be handling too much and therefore stressed so their partner is pushed to compromise.

These are not justifiable reasons. Disobedience to God's order, regardless of the pressure by the enemy is not justified. God's orders remain. God tested the man to know whether or not he would be obedient.

Take time to consider the mentioned stressors, or factors because they could be a test.

Beware; your stress could be a test.

Regardless, God still expects us to be obedient and faithful to the other person. The devil has used these same stressors to make many families fall and separate failing to reach their potentially bright future. One by one, we must apply God's wisdom to each individual case.

On the other hand Eve should not have assumed her husband's responsibility.

Eve went out of her space—out of line for her authority level. The results were chaos in the Garden.

She went out of her space—out of line for her authority level, and she made a decision for her household. The results were chaos in the Garden. And, regardless of the reasons for disobedience, the whole first family set in motion the resulting fair share of punishment. No one was exonerated.

Separation and oppression resulted in the neglect of responsibilities finally leading to death and destruction. We see repeats of the same thing today. Neglect of responsibilities has always been the basic cause of: sickness, separation, oppression, depression, homelessness, suicides, and staggering numbers of deaths.

This situation is forcing children to abruptly become adults. Men are sitting at home while their wives work to feed them. Some men are home because of the lack of employment, some agree to baby sit at home while their wives go to work. After a period of time, some wives start having affairs with stronger career oriented men. They may start a pattern of leaving work late, giving excuses at home.

The same thing goes for men who think they have a wife who is not mentally sharp enough or wise enough to share their intellectual status. Some husbands cannot openly receive respect or speak out in their home because they are either not earning enough, as much as, or more money than their wives, or they are unable to find employment. They are not considered bread winners. Whoever makes the most money, often talks the loudest. Even so, women despise being seen as a pay check!

Role reversal is madness in today's culture. Women think they want to become leaders over men and vice-versa. Women boast of doing what men can do. We can hardly visually tell who is a woman today. Everything is unisex. Some men look and or dress like they are women. We need to be certain of our role and know who we are and not be concerned about other people or the way they look. Today's families are in trouble, because no one knows who is responsible for what, or to whom. "The reason?" you ask. No role is definite. Anyone can just do whatever they like.

Today's families are in trouble, because no one knows who is responsible for what, or to whom. "The reason?" you ask. No role is definite.

God's Purpose Drives A Marriage For A Lifetime

The Biblical role for man is to: provide, care for, protect and promote his wife. Adam promoted Eve when he said, "this is the bone of my bones and flesh of my flesh, she shall be called woman..." The husbandman was the farmer. Husbands grow a crop—their wives! The Biblical role of the woman is to support, help be an influencer to the husband. They were purposed for their tasks and used to be good in their roles!

It is my belief that if this world would follow the only marriage manual, the Word of God; go back to the maker's purpose and set of boundaries; and, take their marriage responsibilities seriously; then, the world would gradually improve toward good. Perhaps at that point another garden would be created and no one would ever talk with the devil or pay attention to his evil advice.

Summary:
- ➤ The union of marriage is often called an institution—The reasoning is that there is a building with a foundation in the Holy Bible. Even the blueprint for carrying on marriage is expanded like a blue print for happiness. It leads to strong homes designed and purposed to last a lifetime.
- ➤ The purposed roles of husband and wife are clearly given in the Word. Review them as set forth in this chapter. Ponder your view compared to the Bible's.
- ➤ The wife is to unconditionally respect her husband and honor him as God's choice for her purposes.
- ➤ Responsibility for the home is to be a joint, by-laterally shared effort. It will require effort of the wife and husband in Christ.
- ➤ The husband is to make difficult decisions and bear responsibility for those choices even when they are not the best ones.

Purpose Driven Marriage

> ➤ Beware of patterning your marriage after your role model family. They could be other than God's perfect pattern. Changing is very difficult, but possible.
> ➤ What Adam did, not making such an important decision in the garden, can cause role reversals in your home and result in serious problems.
> ➤ Tests come in many different forms. Watch out for tests with prayer, Bible study and fellowship within your family.

Questions to Focus on Chapter 7 Insight:
1. What two things should a prospective husband and wife make certain they have?
2. To whom is a married couple responsible, accountable?
3. What are the duties of a husband to his wife?
4. Why is being faithful difficult for so many husbands? Why didn't the wife see and guard his eyes?
5. Are there role problems at your home?
6. What is the Biblical role of the husband? Of the wife?

Chapter 8
Intimacy in Marriage

The letter "I" in Marriage will be used to stand for Intimacy.

Intimacy in marriage does not mean a one-night stand or a hurried short time sexual encounter. There should be no time limit; nor should it be a one sided-enjoyment with the other partner feeling pressured or used.

It is not meant to be used as power to control or as grounds for seeking attention. Any person outside covenanted marriage is able to choose to have a sexual relationship but it is without true intimacy.

Sexual relationship outside covenanted marriage is not true intimacy.

A time of intimacy is not the place for displaying macho-muscle flex, nor should it be abusive. It is a place of purity and dignity where heart-to-heart emotions are displayed, and where free-will in union is dignified. It may not always be sexual exchange. Think about this scenario. Visualize a couple working on different projects yet with each other, silently enjoying the comfort of the loved one's presence. Couples could use this time as a sharing moment listening to each other's stories and emotional wishes or interests. The shame of the words, "don't you see?" or "don't say trite things!" are not allowed within this intimate moment. Intimacy is a language of emotion; it is far beyond the little kisses given to each other in the morning. Words like sweetheart, honey, sugar, darling or words like "I love you" are all good words that could emphasize a degree of intimacy but still they may be used without intimacy in marriage.

Biblical intimacy speaks about the purposed uniqueness of physical oneness and the knowledge of that sacred oneness in the image of God. Different functions are pursued yet amazingly, achieved as though there was one person. The uniqueness of two persons flows into 'one flesh.' What a mystery! Intimacy is the infusion of one person into the other person's flesh-body, uniting the soul-mind and spirit—working together as one. One accepts what the other offers and vice versa. Each of them has something to offer and something to receive with simplicity and appreciation.

The word "intimacy" is a paradigm used by Jesus responding to one of his disciples. He was asked, "...show us the Father" and Jesus answered, "If you have seen Me you have seen the Father. I am in Him and He is in Me, the words that I speak are from Him." John 14:8 KJV

God's Purpose Drives A Marriage For A Lifetime

Often the Bible asks us to be in intimate relationship with God. Instead we treat Him the same way we treat our partners; that is, we become sober, simple, and aloof except when we are in need of something from Him.

This is how many couples treat their relationship. A partner may be looking for attention from the other—by any means—and does whatever is necessary to satisfy it. It is a demand that the particular desire be fulfilled even when it is at the expense or cost of the other person. The demanding partner does not really care. This type of relationship is not an intimate relationship. It is rather a selfish goal met by means of a demanding ultimatum.

Let me delimit what intimacy is in a Christian, or any successful marriage. Intimacy is not a one-night stand, or a hurried fulfillment of physical need by sexual consummation. Marriages today are mostly based on this sexual consummation, with passion and lusting. This God-given grace of pleasure and fulfillment has become a glandulous modern perversion for lusts and worldly ideas. It has come to include practices that are lustfully engaged in enraged behaviors. The flesh is gratified but the spirt of each partner is left isolated. If these acts are not done to the taste of the other partner, the marriage suffers or ends. All kinds of abuse and negativity then may begin. Accompanying this is unnecessary emotional stress, outbursts, rages and surface anger. The home over time becomes cold and foreign to warmth. In this cold, uninteresting place; children begin to feel and see division. They are surrounded by strife and unpleasant words are thrown at them. This happens because one partner—or both of them—has lost the meaning and the power of intimacy.

Sexual exchange, in this defiled relationship could become defiled and far from pure. Ten to twenty minutes of copulation result. The unique time of sensitivity that defines the genuineness of that relationship is corrupted. One does not need intimacy or relationship to have a one-night stand. The world has always offered this perverted accessible sex to any worldly person. Intimacy is not grounds for monopoly of an individual's self-gratification. Nor is it a place for either the husband or wife—particularly the man—to justify selfish interest and pleasure at the expense of their spouse. But, ideally, they will share and enjoy the moment together as a means of appreciating each other.

Intimacy in marriage, which has become consistently selfish, is not meant to be used as a means for power control of the other. In most selfishly controlled type relationships the woman, or the party who is controlled, believes that this time together is their only payback time. They think it is the only time to: get the other person to listen; or make the other person agree on an irresolvable issue. Sex is not to be used as a drug of delusion. According to Confucius, "Sex is the opiate of the masses." Such wrong use affects the mental faculties of the other person. It should not be used as a means of punishment. Yes! It must be mutually agreed upon; but, not a weapon for forcing one's way or will upon the other person. If this becomes the norm, the marriage and the sacred meaning of intimacy will lose its values and dignity. What God purposed and intended the sexual union to do will not be accorded to the partners.

Intimacy that provides a platform for gaining an audience to cheer lead or applaud a meaningful atmosphere for celebrating muscle flexes or macho abusive behaviors, is not a Godly relationship. Nor is it a relationship where God is the center. Is this not the world system? There is no space for violence and abnormal characteristics in the Godly intimate moment. If this occurs, this union should be considered abnormal, a surgical moral—spiritual operation is necessary. Counseling and prayer are strongly suggested in order to begin resolving this abnormality.

Intimacy will not always have to result in the conception of babies, painful relationships, dysfunctional homes, or abandoned children. We should use God's wisdom in our intimate relationship as basis for thinking of the pros and cons of bringing children into the family. Having a large family that we are barely able to financially take care of is not wise for the children. Children are a heritage given to us by God and are special blessings when they are born of intimacy. There are many factors involved in this bond for properly taking care of, nurturing and administering child discipline. Lack of children or adoption of children should not disturb the power of intimacy in marriage. Just because the woman cannot conceive or the man cannot sire children does not close the door to intimacy. Actually, this lack may stimulate a healthy relationship. God is the giver of children. Although there are modern ways of aiding pregnancy and conception of babies, any healthy couple must have God give them directions for His proper way to handle their own unique situation.

This time and emotional moment of intimacy is a place where one's weaknesses are shared: mentally, emotionally, spiritually and physically. There is openness to each other's feelings; one becomes emotionally naked, open to speak the plain truth. Admittance of one's faults to each other—just as we would to God—enables us to enjoy the forgiving attribute of God towards each other. Intimacy heals and is the best solution. The Holy Bible says in Genesis 2:25, "Adam and Eve were both naked and were not ashamed." In I Corinthians 7:3-5 Paul said, neither of the couple should have power over the other's body; that, each party is to surrender his/her body to the other. At this point, everything is surrendered to each other. The potential is a time of refreshing and awesome time of regaining one's self. It seems to me the very pleasant moment of meaningful rest. A rest from: stress, names, what has been, or what should be, but a place to forget one's hurts and to show appreciation of one's love blessings. Let us take this into a more spiritual realm.

> ***This God loved man with an eternal love and, loving him, called him into existence.***
> ***He has given man and marriage both natural and supernatural life.***

The intimate union of husband and a wife indicate the embodiment of God's love. God is love, everything He does—both in and outside Himself—is a work of love. Being the infinite good, He cannot love anything outside of himself. He embodies love and the desire to increase His happiness; and in Himself, He possesses all. This God loved man with an eternal love and, loving him, called him into existence. He has given man and marriage both natural and supernatural life.

The same image we possess as husband and wife are reflected in these same intimate characteristics. Intimacy is what the world describes as romance. Romantic relationship has become "roughmatic" union with irregularities, lack of everything, and ending with the liturgy of "I am sorry." Because of the winding down of time and space, intimate times may be fleeting; yet with effort and purpose we may make time frequently enough to develop this beautiful fellowship of coitus. We can spiritually retreat within ourselves to meet with each other sacrificially before God.

Marriage today is often crippled by anxiety instead of invigorated through stimulating intimacy afforded when the Biblical principle of God's purposed fellowship is applied. God must joyfully become the center of intimacy between husband and wife. This facilitates leaving a Godly example to the children at home (Isaiah 54:10). Intimacy cherishes covenant. It reactivates and keeps covenant at the fore front of relationship.

Every form of Christian life requires the desert, at least to some extent. The desert experience is one of mortification, penance, and giving up of conveniences for the purpose of enriching us in God's likeness.

Our time of intimate relationship with God could be referred to as our "desert place." The spirituality of the desert encourages and stimulates recollection and silence. This setting makes us open to listen to God, and ready to contemplate His mysteries.

Intimacy is an act of silence. Although a relationship between man and woman requires dialogue and speech, talking must not go so far as to incapacitate us for keeping quiet and listening to each other. Silence, which leads to internal reflection, makes us more able to listen, focus, digest and understand others. During this time, we learn to reflect on our mistake, behaviors, and actions. It could be used as a powerful tool to heal any partner's wounds. Silence is an act of discipline geared to produce repentance or positive reactions to one another's unconscious actions.

Foolish conversation and unbridled talkativeness do not open the way to intelligent, persuasive dialogue, suited to bringing the needed word of God into the relationship (household). Intimate time between husband and wife involves each spouse's feelings, memories and impressions. It is an important place of retreat. It is vitally important that the presence of God and the principle of His word saturate the atmosphere of such holy intimacy.

The silence of the presence of God and His Word must saturate the atmosphere of intimacy.

Christian homes have fallen into an idolatry of temporal things. The result is Christian homes have become filled with idolaters and slaves, rather than masters over things and servants to God. Yes, we claim to have the idea by form but actually we deny the powered purpose that would visibly manifest His power through us.

The situation you face is crucially important for family health. If quality time for developing the setting to implement intimacy is given back to your relationship, your family will be healthy—as it should be. The intimate time is ordained by God. His purpose ordered it. It should be. God will enrich your marriage through your obedience to this act.

Summary:
- ➢ Intimacy may be defined as a time of deep sharing in purity and dignity where heart to heart emotions

are shared mentally, emotionally or physically.

- ➤ Physical oneness signifies the "one flesh" infusion of two covenanted beings.
- ➤ Purity and covenant are of highest value in true intimacy. Both wives and husbands are responsible for maintaining Biblical principles in their home.
- ➤ Intimacy was God's plan and we will need effort and determination to keep our lives pure before God.

Questions to Focus on Chapter 8 Insight:
1. What different forms may true intimacy take within marriage?
2. Why are macho and abusive actions not intimacy?
3. Try to explain why words alone are not able to express the union and result in our calling out for the demonstration of true covenanted intimacy of marriage?
4. How can we be intimate with God?
5. Why do some join conception of children with sexual intimacy? What does the Bible indicate? Marriage is the right situation for rearing children, isn't it?
6. What does marital intimacy picture? Does God approve of sexual intimacy that is kept pure and undefiled as he commanded in Hebrews 13:4 AMP?
7. How can the Christian home become filled with slaves and idols?
8. What actions can you take to get your marriage intimacy to Bible standards?

Chapter 9

Accountability

The Letter "A" in marriage will stand for Accountability.

Be thankful to God that we have accountability. The first instruction given to man after his creation was God's teaching about his accountabilities. God taught Adam what He required regarding his responsibilities towards his surrounding, his accommodation, and his wife. Man was accountable to God, while originally woman was accountable her husband.

At the time of the fall from innocence, the blame game started.
Adam blamed Eve. Eve blamed the serpent.

God's Purpose Drives A Marriage For A Lifetime

The serpent got judged for helping the devil.

At the fall from creation's design purpose, both of them become accountable to each other. Man was to take care of and provide for his wife by work—labor, producing sweat. The woman was to encourage, help him make things work, care for daily needs, affirm, and endorse her husband. It was interesting that when man fell, he blamed it on his woman. The woman in turn, blamed it on the serpent. The serpent had no one to blame except his own bad choice, because satan tricked him into being used for evil and this resulted in the serpent's fallen state.

The woman actually was the source through whom the fall came. The man condoned then joined in on woman's choice to eat and later reflected and referred to the awful effects of the fall. The serpent was accountable to God for his actions; therefore, he was held to accountability to Jesus, the seed of the woman. The seed of the woman was identified as the one who would be the instrument of death, bruising his head. The serpent (actually satan) was to strike the heel of the seed of the woman. Striking means he would cause problems, hindrances and pains for human beings. (We often see examples of this in the circles of the ungodly. Surely the enemy continues doing a great job of deception.)

Marriage could be defined as accountability—accountability to each other, to God.

Marriage could be defined as accountability. In marriage, couples are to be accountable to each other. Accountability will require subjectivity of the egos of both persons. More specifically it means both partners are given opportunities to reflect on each other's reports and actions in relationship to God's purpose.

Accountability means general oversight of each other's actions without feelings of shame or guilt.

Accountability controls so that there will not be too much freedom which could cause enslavements in relationship. It keeps the relationship in focus and makes both of the couple work harder to make things happen in the home.

Accountability Summed Up

Accountability in marriage is an expression of the positive forms of the following 'R' words. When the negative 'R' words come into action—watch out, there is danger! These are: receptivity, reflection, rebuttals, rejection, resentment, relocation, and maybe, removal.

Receptivity: Accountability means that information is received. The received information is indicative of peace and orderliness in the house. The received information is then processed and mirrored back to the other partner through attitudes and actions. Received information may be instructional or a feed back on issues and subjects discussed. In case of Adam and Eve, it was a convicting sentence of judgment received by Adam for his engagement and participation in their rebellion against God. The information from either side must be received before the next stage which is reflection may be entered.

Many couples experience problems receiving or accepting information from each other. It is only the information received from the other partner that is possible to be processed in reflection. When the information is graciously received, it will be reflected upon.

Reflection: Individual's reflections on how to handle the information provided enables accountability within the family. Reflection on different issues, especially, sensitive issues in the family help to diagnose possible solutions for struggles and family confusions. Many couples do not reflect on actions or statements they make. This always has adverse effects on their partner. Laxities, neglects, abuses in relationships often result when there is improper handling of positive reflection concerning how others are being affected. Reflection is better when both parties are involved. The individual needs to be given the space to think and reflect on issues affecting the family.

Rebuttal: Reflection results in rebuttal. Rebuttal is dependent upon an individual's ability or willingness to appraise and talk about situations, especially ones that are difficult to deal with. Both parties speak their minds without mental or psychological enslavement or fear of rejection. In other words, both husband and wife must talk things over and allow each other to express their emotional feeling about any given situation. Positive reflection is interactive. Rebutting is an open conversation. It is an honest analysis of processed information. Neither one of the couple is keeping silent. This gives vital health to the relationship. If there is a problem in rebuttal, resentment will result.

Resentment: Honest rebuttal in the house between married partners may at times causes resentment. It results either from wrong presentation or aggressive receptivity. An example of a problem is: one of the partners may in a passive way have been bossed around by the other partner or forced to comply with perceived rules from the spouse. One felt the other should have considered them when making the decision or taking the steps. The solution comes when both parties compromise, work with each other, and handle their emotions before the issues shift to rejection of each other. A sense of accountability within the couple helps to minimize frictions in this case and eases away any tinges of resentment.

Rejection: Some rejections are given out silently, in passive ways through ignoring or not noticing. It may become open rebellion and open confrontation. Many families are living under the bitter agony of lack of accountability. Neither of the parties believed they are accountable to each other. Most believe that it is a gender issue. They think women are always required by culture to be accountable to the husbands. Be reminded the husband did not make the home alone. Both are accountable to each other, and nothing is exempted. Once couples begin to reject each other's view, communication, or ideas, this indicates there is silent trouble in the home.

God's Purpose Drives A Marriage For A Lifetime

Relocation: If there is rejection, the couple may come to the point where neither of them wants to stay together. Each join in playing the game of avoidance and give excuses for not relating to the other. Resentment starts and they separate themselves from each other. This distancing is a sign of a degenerating relationship. The precipitating evil from the decay results in biological separation—husband moves to another bedroom and their chemistry no longer works. Next the game of favoritism begins as a cover up. These are preferences of children; children are torn between love for two parents; and, each child begins to side with their favorite parent. Then financial separation becomes obvious. The accounts are separated—if they ever had a joint account. Next comes moving out of the immediate house. This is for the sake of peace and to avoid physical or mental abuses—if it is not already occurring in the house. At this point the disintegrating family becomes torn apart and other invaders begin to take possession of their union. Everyone now makes his or her own, separate decision without consulting the other partner. They now live separately and the last stage removal begins.

Removal: This is the last stage of the unaccountable relationship. Removal means divorce. First the couple removes themselves emotionally. This causes them to give their attention to work, children, or another person. They may leave the failing relationship for another. This is a shameful stage. It all happened because they failed to be accountable to each other. Everyone claimed individual rights and no one seemed to be patient enough to go through the stages without getting out of harmony. Changes in position, career opportunities, financial increase or decrease, and all kinds of tests come along to test the couple's accountability to each other. The wrong concept stated in today's language is "I am no body's baby sitter." This statement lacks the proper accountability. This mind set will not be able to maintain the couple in a marriage that exemplifies the purpose for a marriage and the resulting home.

The presence of the negative 'R' words is indicative of the lack of accountability within faltering homes. Couples who seek God's purpose will want to pay attention to any signs of weaknesses in any of the stated 'R's. Husband and wife are designed to be accountable to each other. This is how God created marriage in the garden and expanded His instructions after the fall of man. It was the lack of this purpose and knowledge in our relationship with Him that resulted in the separation and destructions of the original human kingdom. In today's marriages we must be accountable to each other to have a meaningful and fulfilling covenant relationship.

Summary:
- Accountability started when God taught Adam about it in the garden—before Eve was gifted to him. God knew the coming choice Adam would need to make.
- Accountability changed after the fall from innocence to accountability.
- God told the story of how He would bring mankind back into intimate relationship with Him through Jesus' gift at the cross of Calvary and resurrection power.
- Accountability in marriage (positive or negative) is an expression of the following 'R' words. These are: receptivity, reflection, rebuttals, rejection, resentment, relocation, and maybe, removal.

> A husband, with the full support of his wife is responsible for guarding and nurturing the coming generations. They remain accountable to God.

Questions to Focus on Chapter 9 Insight:
1. Why do you think Adam chose to eat the fruit—when he knew he was accountable to God and disobeying? (Do we understand holy, pure love?)
2. Who is responsible for accountability in the home?
3. If you don't receive information, can you be accountable anyway?
4. Do you and your mate honestly reflect on, think deeply upon, problem areas?
5. What do you do when your mate rejects or rebuttals your plan?
6. List honestly any resentment you have in your heart toward your mate. What will happen if you do not forgive them and work out a solution?
7. Do you ever ignore your mate and give them the "silent" treatment?
8. Rejecting your mate could eventually lead to what? (Oh, no, not that!)
9. What is the path to relocation and removal of a mate?
10. Have you prayed and fasted and sought the Father God's loving heart toward your mate? Remember, you chose them from the many fish in the lake of life.

Chapter 10

Giving

Giving: Body, Soul, & Spirit

The letter "G" is another letter from within marriage that reveals more of the purpose within the total meaning God intended in marriage, Giving.

Let us set the foundation of this topic in the word of God, Ephesians 5:25 says "Husbands love your wives, even as Christ also loved the church, and gave himself for it."

Please notice the comparison of loving and giving of Jesus to the church, and the husband loving and giving himself to the wife. In Galatians 2:20 Paul says, "I am crucified with Christ, nevertheless, I live; yet not I but Christ lives in me, and the Life which I now live in the flesh I live by the faith of the son of God, who loved me and gave himself for me." Please notice Jesus Christ was given by Himself for us.

Focus accurately; we are dealing with family, the husband and wife relationship. The foundation of this family unit should be firmly dependent upon the Creator and His principles revealed in the Word of God—not the worldly standard. I Timothy 2:6 says "Jesus gave himself a ransom for all to be justified in due time."

How is giving demonstrated in the marriage relationship? Giving is: a sacrificial surrendering of one's self; yielding one's life to another without strings attached and without intent of getting something back. It is not what you do to get from the other person but what you purpose to do as a voluntary service for the other person. In this kind of giving you don't expect returns. If there is some return, appreciate it do not abuse it. Although return comes as a reward, this return is not a payback for the purposeful giving of self to Christ or to another. God's purpose is to implement pure sacrificial giving within marriage.

God's purpose was to incorporate sacrificial giving into marital love—like He did with Jesus.

Relationship suffers under the microscope of non-believers' definition of "give and take" syndrome. The quote "you give to receive," yes naturally, is acceptable. It is of interest that this statement indicates the reason we give. Most of us give and expect, as does the world, to receive something back in return. This is not the right definition for giving in relationships, but this error is what today family is and the basis for relationships. We've noted that this idea

Purpose Driven Marriage

is costing dearly in damage to homes. Chaotic society is the end result of 'give to get' thinking.

Currently Christian homes have been so thoroughly indoctrinated by this same principle that their children have engaged themselves in the same mentality. The idea of give and take brings detriment to their lives both in and outside their homes. Many men walk into their new marriage family with this mindset, just to find out that the idea is odd to their new wife and vice visa. Immediately the marriage begins to need patching and mending because of this philosophy.

When Biblical meaning is applied to giving we see it is to do something sacrificially without expecting returns. Spending time digging into this idea deepens understanding of this Biblical concept, and will rescue today's families from constant breaks. God's purpose is pure love.

Today's marriages are mostly business type contractual marriages. Marriage is based on money and material things. Thinking of what one person could get from the other person consciously or unconsciously is what now pervades marriages. Similarly, many people erroneously claim to be Christian because of what they want to get out of God, not because they really love Him. They are Christians to satisfy their needs. By comparison many people go into the marriage relationship, not out of love, but as a means to justify meeting their needs.

These errors in purpose are causing today's marriage relationships to become institutions for exploitation. The marriage, it is thought, is where individuals run to grab and to exploit the other—weaker or more giving individual—be it the man or the woman. Conversely, the purpose of God is self giving love.

God's Purpose Drives A Marriage For A Lifetime

Marriage is supposed to be an institution that promotes charity. It is designed to show Godly giving where the husband gives all, and the wife surrenders to and unconditionally supports her husband. Modern family relationships are so frightful that, the husband finds it hard to trust his wife and the wife tries to do what she can to defend herself. In case anyone lacks purpose and changes their mind on the spur of the moment, who suffers? The children do. And society picks up the mess. Some children may be so badly damaged that they may become teen parents, alcoholics, drug addicts, or prostitutes. These addictions are usually fueled by the idea that says, "Whatever I give, I must get something in return." God's purpose is unseen in this mind set.

Wrong teaching as we have mentioned has caused lack of trust between husband and wife. I know of many families that refuse to have a joint account with their spouses. They have separate accounts, separate cars, separate upbringing, separate background, separate causes, separate closets, but a common bed. They have many separated ideas and actions. They have only one common cause, 'The Bed,' unites them. Should this be considered a healthy relationship or a Biblical purpose driven Christian family pattern? According to Hebrews 13:4, the answer is emphatically, No!

Couples no doubt have often come from different life styles where they were raised in different settings with unique values and exposed to various ethnic upbringings. Some arise from non-Christian cultures and even speak different languages. I am aware of multicultural marriages, but the Biblical purpose and principle remains unchanged. The Bible says that, when a man and woman agree to marry, they are no longer two but become one. Each person has relinquished their right to the other—absolutely—without going back or looking backward.

The husband gives up his family; that is, his focus moves to allegiance to his mate, so he gives total attention to his wife. The same is true for the wife. Unfortunately, there are many couples who are still married to their extended families. The husband is still attached to his family, while the wife still gets advice from her mother. In such relationships they remain directed by separate entities. Neither of them, in this type situation has given up giving attention to self, nor have they bonded to work as a capable unit in the flow of God's purpose. Something else is individually driving them.

Giving means, both husband and wife share equal ownership of self in everything. It means giving total attention to God's purpose and each other. Giving our body, soul and spirit in every possible way enables God's purpose to empower family succeed.

Without mutual total giving of one's self, one or the other of the couple will begin to feel insecure. Other dynamics often bring one to think less of so as to perceive an advantage over the other partner. One may have a better education, more advantage in a position at work, or garnered more riches than the other person. Instead of them seeing differences as a purposeful complement, they see it as a threat. Insecurity, inferiority complex, and unnecessary anxieties develop, thereby causing withdrawal and mood changes aborting God's purposes.

According to the Bible, giving is the ability to surrender one's gifts; talents, and ability totally to the support and development of the other partner. God's purpose in giving does not see a reason for pay back. Jesus gave His life a ransom for all. He then gave human beings the choice either to accept Him or reject Him. Truly, He loves us very much! The Bible said while we were still in our sins, He loved us.

The husband is to give everything to enable him to satisfy his wife. This purpose is true regardless of how the wife treats him. The wife is to give all she is or has to her husband. This honors God, and that is good for they will give account to Him. In a healthy Christian home, position, talents, or money should not be a force setting the terms for offering of one's self to their partner. This harmful attitude permeates our non-believing world. Giving means sacrificially purposing to give to the other person—not as an obligation—but a service, while believing that both of you will account to God for your gifts.

Giving means we, as a couple, have purposed to lose ourselves to the good of the other mate.

The reason we should give attention to this reciprocal giving is that both the husband and wife are to give to each other. Where only one is giving purposefully and sacrificially without the contribution by the other there may be results we do not want. These may be our: need for attention, support, counseling, prayer or strong divine intervention. If our mind is set to believe what the scripture says about marriage then we must both expect to give full energy and vitality to our relationship. There can be no calculated price tagged to the giving that follows God's purpose.

Giving of ourselves to each other means, we have purposed to lose ourselves to the good of the other person. We no longer think impurely or act selfishly. We act in the interest of the other person. The husband takes care of the wife as he would take care of himself, his wife does the same. Each accepts the strengths and weaknesses of the other. Individual gifts or lack of gifts does not matter. Position or lack of it is of no importance. Both embrace the struggles within the house. Name calling and passing blames for competency or incompetency is now taboo. Money and health—the two loud speakers in the family—become controllable with the keys of ferverently praying and the Holy Spirit's intervention. Greed and pride exit to find another place to make their victory celebration.

We must give according to the Word of God. In bygone years, husbands worked to provide for the needs of the family, but today, both partners usually have to work to provide for the family. Yet Christian couples should plan to create a time to give to one another and the children. This effort will insure stability and healthy family growth. This Biblical idea of giving is important in the family of today. We must face the reality and fact that the lack of this genuine, sincere, and God purposed giving makes a mockery of marriages in our society.

Summary:
- ➢ Giving like Jesus gave to benefit the church is the basis for covenanted marriage.
- ➢ Though each marriage partner gives all—they are living through the life of the other member of their "one flesh" union. So we live in Christ's stead.

- ➢ Any marriage based on the world premise of 'give to get' thinking will have immediate problems. Only through knowing Christ's example may we learn the power of giving without though of our benefit.
- ➢ To enter marriage to meet your need is a wrong reason for marriage for a Christian.
- ➢ Wrong teachings gendered problems when couples never amalgamate their lives into a consistent one purpose flow.
- ➢ Biblical principles apply even in multicultural marriages.
- ➢ Giving means both the husband and wife share equal ownership of themselves—in everything within God's purpose.

Questions to Focus on Chapter 10 Insight:
1. Does your marriage show this level of selfless giving?
2. How can you demonstrate sacrificial giving? List some ways.
3. Can God change mindsets that are leading to problems? How?
4. Do you serve God because you love Him, or are you looking to get something He has to offer? (Get real!)
5. What are examples of things a couple will do when they are living separate lives, though they are still married?
6. Who are the usual big losers in the 'give to get' thinking?
7. How can you make your darling mate feel totally secure?

Chapter 11

Enduring Eternal Relationship

The last letter in marriage is "E" and it stands for enduring and eternal relationship.

God created man and woman to live forever. They were not created to die. They were not temporary earth beings. They were created to live and reflect His glory forever. Adam and Eve were to live as husband and wife eternally, but sin cut that short. They were both endorsed for God's purpose of fellowship and eternal life. Sin came in to the garden couple and stopped the lasting arrangement—for a season. Jesus Christ came in the likeness of man to restore our original spiritual status, eternally purposed and called to be married to Christ our Lord.

Any relationship based on God's spirit is strengthened to endure hardships, the devil's temptations, and the tricks of the wilderness. Marriage's purpose is for endurance.

Marriage is partnership to keep the other company till both depart from flesh and continue in their spiritual status in heaven with God. Marriage was designed for endurance, and for keeping covenant relationship between marriage partners. Since man is made in the spiritual image of God (the image that does not die), he is to live forever through the knowledge of God. The partnership between man and woman is designed to last till the end of their physical life here on earth. We may, some feel—not based on scriptures, find family associations still closely aligned in heaven because of spiritual growth.

The marriage 'E' is for endurance, the strength, wisdom and knowledge to manage any situation and not allow the situation to manage us. Endurance is a decision to help, trust in or depend on the help of another person for survival or achievement. Without endurance, marriages cannot last. Many start well and end shortly. Therefore, marriages are strengthened by endurance.

Anyone who beats himself is becoming insane.

Endurance involves experience, experience fosters informed maturity, and maturity produces wisdom for completeness. When one is able to endure their mate's personality, differences, etc., without guilt, the relationship which may at first have been one sided, but will later have meaning and substance to it. Anyway, the marriage is coming to the place past toleration so that the personalities of the mates mesh together. Ideally it will be like the husband looking at himself in the mirror, seeing the image of his wife. The man looks at his completion, which he is in the image of his wife and vice versa. Once the husband cannot beat himself or punch his image he sees in the mirror, then he cannot abuse or punch the wife who is his express image or His glorious reflection. Anyone who beats himself is becoming insane.

Marriage is endurance extended to include one's deformities—in the other partner. Just as one looks into the mirror to correct or make adjustments of himself with patience, so, may one look into the mirror in one's partner to correct, work with, and make adjustments and improvement to the faulty image. We are images of each other's lack.

We need endurance to help each other become the purposed and the exactly perfect being intended by God. Both husband and wife should look at their images in the Mirror of Christ. He is the visible image of the invisible God. It is through this mirror purpose that we can correct our lives and relationships. Here we may make spiritual dresses for the kingdom of God which has no end. Thus, our physical marriage relationship is to be lasting to the end of our lives here on earth. Permanently through our spiritual rebirth and mirrored image's reform—we may perfect it and have it last eternally with the Christ in the Kingdom of God.

Marriage according to the plan of God is supposed to be permanent and lasting. We are to grow in this relationship until death separates us into glory. There is no marriage (as we know it) in the new millennium or in heaven, because we will be like the status of the angels. Knowing this means marriage ends when death takes one of the couple. Marriage starts when the vow is taken and continues until death (the challenge to life), takes one or both of the couple home to Heaven. The Biblical idea of marriage is to encourage a couple to endure.

As long as they are husband and wife divorce or separation are not options for solving marital difficulties. A marriage that functions with Biblical principles showing God's purpose will stay together and work on challenges until their possible solution is achieved and His purpose brings joy.

Today marriages often don't last because of errant worldly perspectives couples bring into their relationships. Almost all marriages, both Christian and non-Christian, are controlled by the 'third party effect.' 'Third party effect' means the marriage is what the other external family or marriage patterns of the family are. What others pattern their family vision around—friends at work—at church— at the movie—or somewhere else, are saying what a family should be. Even news on television, movies, comic books, or glamorizing magazines from a news stand all offer some type of directions as to how families are to be shaped.

Is your marriage patterned after a glamour market failed plan? Why?

Circulars, text books and a little of everything has contributed to the definition of a family. These unholy inputs dictate what the level of our relationship ought to be. The glamorous counterfeit life styles offered in worldly marriages are lies behind the facade which weighs heavily against the functions of God's purpose that drives a successful family. Most of these worldly stereotypes have come from broken homes or ones without a firm home basis. Further, most of them defile basic purpose and

Purpose Driven Marriage

meaning of Biblical relationship. Their only concern is how they can promote and market their failures to struggling families.

The truth of the matter is: There is nothing the devil or his system offers that is ever lasting or eternal. They are temporary fleeting relationships. Imagine what the everlasting relationship in the Garden of Eden could have been. The first separation would not have happened nor the later divorce. Divorce followed and took its terrible toll on humanity. I am sure, as a Christian, we know of the damages. Many have taken years to be re-married or re-united again through the atoning death and resurrection of Jesus Christ. Because, the first couple, Adam and Eve, listened to the devil's trick question and suggestions, man aborted God's purpose for marriage and was expelled—thrown from God's designed position and denied longevity of life in their rebellious sinful state. The result was they were banished from the Garden of God--Eden.

Jesus said Moses authorized the Certificate of Divorce by permission. This was allowed because of the hardness and stubbornness of the people's hearts. (Matthew 19:8. For more information see the entire passage in verses 5-9.) It was not the original intention of God. The original intention of God is that one man and one woman would live together as husband and wife eternally without death, with God's purpose directing a pure, selfless love in perfect peace and harmony.

This means we have a lasting memory of one another in this world, and when one partner dies first, the other carries the memory of that person. Especially they remember the birth of children and grand children. This means they never allow their mate to die. The person may die physically, but spiritually, mentally, psychologically, he or she still lives on. When both of them are no longer living—because of old age—or, premature death—which could be caused by any situation, the memories, and work of the couple and their name still live on in the books of this world. Pictures, books, functions, roles, etc. of family will never be erased in this world until God returns. He will at that time completely terminate the existence of this world either by destroying it by fire or repairing it to establish the new one. But, as long as this world exists, the marriage relationship between man and women was His plan.

Families were to have their records retelling their past by written or oral traditions which are passed as points of reference from one generation to the next. The Bible gave us this picture. The Bible recorded families that were essential to faith. It tells what they did and how they became either a positive or negative role model for their own time and for our world. We read them though their deaths were thousands of years ago; they are preserved by the Word of God. The families of these historical people are retold and living today. Marriage is to be a "forever relationship" as far as time in this world is concerned.

This Biblical purpose of marriage is the aim of today's wise Godly families. The mature couple is meant to live together until death separates them. They are to live as a role model for their children who will carry on, remembering their actions and achievements from one generation to the other. Children keep the name and the union continuing for generations. Marriage according to Bible purpose lasts when it is composed of one Godly man and one Godly woman. Hopefully they are one flesh and not two.

Conversely, if they are separated, two, and both husband and wife are living in this earth, they are Biblically directed to not seek divorce, but stay as one and keep that union until death separates them. Some spouses are prematurely separated by sickness or other means leading to death. Then they may move on to re-marry another person, this of course is permitted by the Word of God. In most cases, problems of the previous marriage carry over into the new relationship. Emotional imbalances will need God's intervention for proper healing. The vital message is: It was death that separated the first marriage, and the memory of that first marriage cannot be erased. This is especially true if children were involved. The remaining marriage partner need not remain single for the rest of his or her life.

Regardless, the memory of the initial marriage lives on and cannot be killed or replaced by a new individual or family union. God has a divine intention and purpose for husband and wife to live together and be happy for life. Any husband and wife should love themselves and pray for God's purpose and a long life to fulfill the divine purpose. He planned for marriage partners to mesh and enjoy themselves, which originally meant He designed them to live together forever.

As you read this book, there may be many questions running through your mind. You might seek reasons why marriages don't last forever. Those reasons are usually permitted by God, but not His perfect will. Most of them are caused by our own selfish, ungodly ambitions in life.

In historic sources, people used to ask God about their spouses, pray for days, months, and years to have God point them to the right person. But now, this is usually not so. Very few of today's young people even have it in their minds to believe God for Christian partners. Formerly, parents used to exercise a Godly, dominant role in appointing mates for their children. Today this idea seems ancient, out dated and an archaic idea. Some avoid it like a taboo. The fear of God used to be the guiding light, and moral family backgrounds used to be the measuring tool. All of this contributed to longer marriages and stable relationships, but today it seems a waste of time and old fashioned. Hardly any Christian considers the purpose behind spiritual homes they would desire to establish and enjoy for the rest of their lives. Christians decide to marry non-Christians, tempting God being under a delusion that they are to lead the other unbelieving spouse to God. Many jump into ungodly relationships. Marriages as a result are breaking apart almost as soon as they are joined together. The result today is a divorce epidemic.

Authorities have licensed all kinds of sodomites. These actions in our condemned and to be destroyed sinful old world are stopping God's brilliant purpose and plan from showing His kind of love in long, happy, stable marriages.

We have to recognize the fact that, relationships of husbands and wives are now based on trial and error. To the contrary, marriage is a serious vow sealed by a blood covenant gravely important before God. When a couple are not ready for the commitments and the challenges it brings, they should postpone their plan or consider not marrying until they are ready.

Divorce or separation breaks not only the family, but also the entire structure and makeup of the individuals involved. Everything breaks down. All types of character behaviors arise after divorce of a love one.

Purpose Driven Marriage

It seems like losing an arm, an eye, or a leg by amputation is bad. But, the damage to one part leaves all parts of the body crippled and imbalanced. It is a lasting disability. Why do it? Why would you want to subject yourself to this excruciating problem, the debilitation of the family and the pain?

You can read the principles guiding marriage and what it means to go through the 'needle's eye' in the scripture and purpose putting your family together. When Bible principles cause you to embrace positive changes, to show tolerance, to detach yourself from worldly advice, and to allow God to take control of your household--your family will regain Godly balance.

The two basic questions that could help marriages are:

- Upon what purpose or foundation is our family structured?
- And, who is confronting the family?

If these two questions could be answered in the true Biblical sense, then the marriage is going to last for a lifetime with eternity remembering. Yes, for all eternity. If any of these questions cannot be answered Biblically, then, it is only a matter of time until it will soon sicken and die (Matthew 19:1-8).

Some have argued that, the same Word of God permits divorce based on the premise of one of the couple's committing adultery. If we based divorce on this passage then, there would be no marriage because the Bible said; everyone who looks lustfully in his heart on the opposite sex in his or her mind has committed adultery. Adultery is a sin from the heart that calls for repentance. To take this passage to mean there is a license for divorce that O.K.'s the sin when an act is committed is justifying the wrong and I believe is error. The party that commits the act lives to marry another person, which is considered adultery. The party who is unfaithful over and over may grossly pollute the family so that no other action than divorce is possible for peace. The innocent partner, if they marry another person, is called fornicator. This is a 'no win' situation—unless true repentance has applied Jesus' blood to the sin.

If you live, because of the fornication, it is better to live without ever marrying again. This is because whoever marries you is committing adultery unless you have truly repented of your broken covenant and find Jesus' grace. The reason that you took the route of divorce is a breach of God's purpose for marriage relationship. In Malachi 2:16 "For the LORD God of Israel says, He hates divorce for it covers one's garment with violence.... Therefore take heed to your spirit that you do not deal treacherously."

This is crucial. The problem of today's marriages is divorce, which is breaking the purpose of covenants and faith. The idea planned by God is that husband and wife live together for a life time, not temporarily. So guard yourself in your spirit. Do not break faith with that purpose for marriage.

Summary:
- ➢ Endurance is a decision to help or trust help from another to gain the goal of lifetime marriage.
- ➢ If you have progressed in your marriage past tolerance to meshing, good work.
- ➢ How does your image look when you look in the Mirror of Christ? Like Christ? Good.
- ➢ Marriage vows end when one partner leaves by death.

Purpose Driven Marriage

- Divorce is not an option, even because of a onetime unfaithfulness. One long time married laughed as he was saying "We once considered murder."—but obviously, they didn't do that.
- Third party effect will call for unrealistic expectations in a marriage and should be avoided and disclaimed.
- Glamorous counterfeit life styles are a façade that destroys Godly purpose for marriages.
- Blood covenant between man and woman is the only Biblical marriage.
- Remarriage always has left over memories; children and fragmented family attached making forgiven successful marriage very difficult to accomplish. God's purpose and design was for one marriage lasting a lifetime. Thank God for the forgiveness in Christ's blood!

Questions to Focus on Chapter 11 Insight:
1. Define endurance?
2. What three factors does endurance involve?
3. Who should the wife see when looking at herself in the mirror?
4. Why would she not see herself?
5. Have you any 'third party effect' showing in your marriage? Who from?
6. What does the devil offer that lasts a lifetime?
7. What was the original plan for Adam and Eve? NEVER DIE?
8. When will the marriage plan end on earth?
9. What are two basic questions that could help marriages?
10. Pinpoint the problem in your marriage and if you are remarried, did you have it before? (Dig deeply within and bypass the guard wall you have set up.)

11. Share how you and your mate became covenant partners.

PART III

APPLYING THE IDEAL PURPOSE TO LIFE AND THE ORDEALS OF SIN

Chapter 12

Functions of Repentance

There IS NO EXCEPTION to the purpose of holiness. We are to be like our God—holy! "Be ye holy, for I am holy!" This is given as a commanded purpose several times in the Bible. (See Matthew 5:48; I Peter 1:16; Psalm 99:9; and Deuteronomy 10:12.)

Man is a sinful creature who needs to apply repentance. He needs to turn and forsake his sinful ways, for he has missed God's demand for holiness. Our flesh pulls us to actions opposite God's holiness. The spirit is truly willing, but as Paul said to the Corinthians (They truly understood sins of the flesh.) in I Corinthians 6:17-20.

"...The person who is united to the Lord becomes one spirit with Him. Shun immorality and all sexual looseness [flee from impurity in thought, word, or deed]. Any other sin which a man commits is one outside the body, but he who commits sexual immorality sins against his own body. Do you not know that your body is the temple (the very sanctuary) of the Holy Spirit Who lives within you, Whom you have received [as a Gift] from God? YOU ARE NOT YOR OWN, You were bought with a price [purchased with preciousness and paid for, make His own]. So then, honor God and bring glory to Him in your body." I Corinthians 6:17-20 AMP with possible extended translations shown in brackets.

Again, this was Paul admonishing a very sinful people—just like we are today.

According to this study we have learned that our natures are corrupted by sin. Therefore, we can no longer function without the Spirit of God within us. It was this fallen nature that separated us from God's purpose starting in the garden. The effect of that separation is still lingering in families today. Instead of life time marriages many are experiencing painful short time mini-marriages.

The Effects of Sin Ended Your Marriage

When we are not holy—sin begins and sin will end even the greatest Godly and potentially wonderful purpose driven marriage. Sin unchecked and not faced as such will kill purpose and sink any ship of marriage! Confession and changing to God's purpose is the only hope for marriages with problems. And—the only remedy for those who are already divorced is sincere repentance coupled with forgiveness.

Repentance Begins at Jesus' Feet. Separate yourself from normal activities and seek to read some New Testament scriptures, probably from the book of John while reflecting upon what has brought you to this point in your walk with Jesus.

God's Purpose Drives A Marriage For A Lifetime

Spend a period of time asking God for insight into holiness and confessing your own shortcomings. Focus on God's strength and personal weaknesses. Review Bible principles and forgive yourself and adopt God's purposes. Dwelling on your failures will bring mourning if you stay there too long, but tears of true repentance will cleanse you body, soul and spirit.

Remember, He promised and He's not a man that He should fail. So, "If we confess our sins, He is faithful and just to forgive us our sins and cleanse us from ALL UNRIGHTEOUSNESS." I John 1:9 NKJ

"Come unto Me (Jesus), all you who labor and are heavy laden, And I will give you rest." Matthew 11:28

Time invested in fellowship and prayer will restore your communication with the Lord. To develop a friendship you will need to spend time in prayerful study of the Bible and talk with the Lord Jesus as a friend sitting next to you. Tell Him you only want His responses—not from any other and expect Him to gently respond inside you. That's where He lives by the presence of the Holy Spirit within us.

There is no quick fix for any pattern of sin. Practice a positively holy action 20 to 30 times and you will replace any formerly unwanted bad habit of words, response or thought. Work at the changes one by one. Avoid self accusations. Compliment yourself for any change. Celebrate Jesus' gift at Calvary and the work of the Holy Spirit within during this time of clearing the patterns of the world.

Reinstall God's purpose and start implementing His purpose. Start today with prayer seeking, begging and asking for personal forgiveness. Remember, He said you would be heard when you repent of stubborn sins and really change your direction toward the pattern shown in the Bible.

Be aware and don't mourn too long; Jesus' arms are waiting to comfort a truly repentant soul. "Come unto Me and I will give you rest." What a comforter the Holy Spirit is.

Summary:
- The command to be Holy for I am holy is given many times in the Bible. God meant it. Be Holy. He wouldn't tell you if you couldn't do it.
- The Holy Spirit within enables us to change bit by bit. You are the temple of God. With repentance comes forgiveness!
- Our flesh has a tendency to pull us into sinning. Resist and don't go.
- A broken covenant—your choice or not—is a breach of covenant. God hates divorce. It messes up our life and He requires repentance.
- Don't grieve so long that you are overpowered by mourning and depression's heaviness. Remember, Jesus' blood washes sins away. We have a better covenant than the Old Covenant. Our sins are washed away—GONE!

God's Purpose Drives A Marriage For A Lifetime

> ➢ Restore God's plans and purpose to your life starting as soon as you feel His peace flood your soul.

Questions to Focus on Chapter 12 Insight:
1. Pray about the areas you need to visit spiritually and cover with true repentance.
2. Do you have a mental list of the ones who have hurt you? Take them to Jesus at the Cross—leave them there for Him to take care of. Don't go back and pick them up or tell Jesus how to take care of them.
3. How long did you need to pray to have the list leave your thoughts? Pray until they go.
4. Is your desire for intimacy still at an elevated level? Pray and ask God to take even normal desire from you, until you need it, so you can have peace in this area. [Some of you have just been set free from a sexual addict and need deliverance from the Spirit of Harlotry and the Spirit of Perversion, etc. Ask Jesus to come with His Spirit of Agape' Love and The Spirit of Awe of God to push out the yucky two. If you need more help see the footnote.[2] Expect some battling in prayer, but you will gain victory. Others have gained victory in this area and all praises go to Jesus for that!
5. Are you attending church with strong Bible believing Christians? No? Why not?
6. Fellowship with the Lord is essential and fellowship with believers is too.

---

2. From Thumb Sucking to Tabret Dancing Myrna L. Goehri Etheridge, 2002, M. Etheridge Publishing, ISBN 0-937417-16-5. Break Forth Into JOY 2nd Ed., by Myrna L. Goehri Etheridge, M. Etheridge Publishing, 1992 ISBN 0-937417-12-2, Contact: Email:myrnae@onemain.com, or www.gmeministries.org

7. Are you doing what Jude, (natural brother in Jesus' family) 20 tells us to do? Pray without ceasing in the Holy Spirit. "But you, beloved, build yourselves up [founded] on your most holy faith [make progress, rise like an edifice higher and higher], praying in the Holy Spirit." AMP Jude 20 If not read the entire book of Acts out loud and then ask for the baptism with the Holy Spirit. Jesus is faithful to baptize us, if asked.

Chapter 13

Mercy and Grace for Marriages

God meets our desire out of His great love and mercy! There is unearned affection lavished toward you. Boundless favor is flowing toward you. Receive it though no action has been given. Without a single thing we have or could have done to base it upon, nor is it what we deserve yet we have His mercy and grace. All these benefits were afforded to us in the gift of Jesus Christ.

He loved us though we were lost in sin. The Father God sent his only son to earth to become the gift of eternal life to each person who will accept the gift.

If Jesus isn't living and resident Lord of your life, please, request His presence and yield to His life giving presence.

Living for Him will never be less than eternally exciting and a challenge for Holy living. And, with Holy Spirit's power helping you, there is overcoming power. Invite Jesus in. Do it right now.

God's love is toward us, even in our sinful choices. His love is without reference to our qualifications. He loves because He created and gave live to us. You can't earn this love. Neither can you make it go away. As was stated earlier in this book, "Think on that for a few days!"

All this is about unearned and enduring love for you from your creator—designer. His love for you is just because you are—not earned. Please, spend a couple more days to think on that! Meditate on John 3:16-18. "For God so loved the world that he sent his only begotten son…"

God's love for us started before the world was created— when we were in his heart of love. So don't worry. We can't lose His love. This is a paraphrase of Ephesians 1:4

In its final essence marriage ideally equals the purpose displayed on earth for the example of the Father-Son-Holy Spirit's mercy and grace. The example of His grace was shown in Jesus Christ our Savior and Lord.

God's Purpose Drives A Marriage For A Lifetime

Marriage has an eternal purpose of displaying God's character on earth. There is no other visible earthly example of the Triune Nature of Jehovah God on the earth outside of Christian joyful marriage and family.

"Mercy and truth are met together and righteousness and peace have kissed" Psalms 85:10 NKJ

"His mercy is new every morning." Lamentations 3:23

"I will sing of mercy and judgment…" Psalm 101:1

"Mercy triumphs over judgment…" James 2:13

"The son of man has come to seek and to save that which was lost" Luke 19:10 NKJ

His mercy is new every morning. (Paraphrase of Psalm 59:16.) Mercy and Grace kissed each other when Jesus' gift was given to us at Calvary.

He promised if you would seek Him with all your heart, you would find Him. His mercy will be with him. He loves you unconditionally. He extended His mercy and grace so we may receive of His nature and live for His glory.

Purpose Driven Marriage

"According as he hath chosen us in him before the foundation of the world, that we should be holy and without blame before him in love." Ephesians 1:4 KJV

Summary:
- ➢ The basis of all God's love is His gift of Jesus Christ to redeem fallen man. John 3:16-18 summarizes His view of man and the purposed plan for the future of mankind. That future includes all humans—including us. Celebrate that!
- ➢ Even when we make foolish, even sinful choices—Jesus will forgive when we repent because of His mercy and grace.
- ➢ You can't fall out of God's hand—unless you disown Him and really mean it. Please, don't do that. He's waiting for your heart to come to Him desiring His presence.
- ➢ Each day His mercy is restored to full measure. He knew we'll need that.
- ➢ He's known you since you were in the molten lava of the earth in molecular form. He purposed you would know and serve His purpose even then.
- ➢ Jesus becomes the husband to single women and the bride to single men. He knows your heart and will meet you where you are right now. Pray. Dear Lord Jesus, touch me today and lift the feelings that weigh me down. Give me of your mercy and grace to walk more closely with you each day. Amen.

Questions to Focus on Chapter 13 Insight:
1. How does God know your desires?
2. Why did Jesus choose to love us so much that He would die for us?
3. Once my marriage failed I thought you were angry with me? Why aren't you?

4. Do you understand how mercy and grace kissed on the cross of Calvary?
5. Have you sought God, crying out to him like David said? He promised you would find Him.
6. Do you have any hope left for the future?
7. Jesus can restore hope. Ask Him what His plan is for your life. Listen, and write it down.

Chapter 14

Avoiding the Enduring Effects of Failed Marriage

Every possible effort should be expended to avoid divorce because of the many side effects on the children, family and other people involved. Any purpose failure affects everyone in your world—especially you and the children!

Divorce causes children's support system to suddenly shrink—or end. They may feel they are the reason for the arguments and fights. Guilt overwhelms some of them. Suddenly, their favorite aunt/uncle/cousin is as though they were dead.

One child, a casualty of divorce, shared her first memories were of sitting upon her bed, clutching her favorite stuffed toy, a bear, crying as she was thinking.

"Mommy and Daddy are fighting because I did something wrong. It's all my fault, Fuzzy Bear!" She continued weeping bitter tears of agony for something she in no way caused! These are child victims of adult sin and stubbornness.

God's Purpose Drives A Marriage For A Lifetime

Some remember listening in the womb. Most thumb sucking children are enduring direct results of this family craziness. They are trying to comfort their uneasiness resulting from hearing or witnessing the conflicts or harsh words—thinking they are the reason for the family problems.

Remember God changes:
>Times
>Seasons
>Removes Kings
>Sets up Kings
>Gives Wisdom
>Gives Knowledge
>
>Reveals secret things

And in His great mercy for fallen man, God the Father sent a lamb.

That lamb, the Lamb of God, changed a family in Genesis 3:21 when God covered them with blood and indicated that there had to be a sacrifice for sin to be covered. Yes, even Adam and Eve who had walked with God in the afternoon breeze of the Spirit of God in the garden needed help with their sin.

Next He changed—a nation in Exodus 12:3-17 when all Israel as slaves celebrated the First Passover with the sacrificed lamb's blood covering the sins of a household.— then Jesus came to redeem the world.

Jesus was slain on Passover and washed away the sins of those who chose to believe 1) His sacrifice, 2) His resurrection; and, 3) who Jesus really was. John 3:16-18.

Purpose Driven Marriage

John, the last sacrifice's cousin in the natural world summed it up so beautifully, "Behold the lamb of God who takes away the sins of the world!" John 1:29; 1:32-37 AMP.

We need to follow Jesus too, because He changes circumstances.

Don't be surprised though, if your mountain looks darker—just before DAWN BREAKS THROUGH. It always seems the darkest just before the peace arrives in your heart! Press through your circumstances until God's peace comes into your heart and mind.

BUT GOD! BUT GOD changes darkness to the glory of the new day! The morning will come and the sun will arise within your soul. The process may take time, but it will happen. We've been that way—it does happen when the elements and actions given in this book are carried out. Next comes the beautiful morning!

Keep reading your Bible each day—it's like an IV. It may not have a taste, doesn't feel very good either. But the substance will sustain your spirit and guide your soul.

However, He never alters His eternal purposes! He is eternally one with these same principles. "Jesus Christ (the Messiah) is [always] the same, yesterday, today, [yes] and forever (to the ages)." Hebrews 13:8 AMP

Change to Rejoin God's Purpose

<u>Repent.</u> Be severely grieved for your involvement in the breakdown of purpose leading to the progression ending in divorce. With God's power, the Holy Spirit helping you—determine to regain the purpose of God and forge into a new way of acting within your life.

<u>Forgive.</u> Regardless of whose "fault" the crash was the tears will continue until you forgive as you continue to seek God's peace. There will most likely be bitter tears and deep sadness. Before God's peace and renewed purity flood your soul the grace to turn lose of the right to get even will free your emotions. Then your mind, will and emotions will enter a time of recovery. Forgiveness brings freedom to enter God's loving peace. Forgive yourself and those who have caused hurt. This process often comes full circle in about two years. Those years need to be filled with prayer, fasting and probably tears that cleanse the hurts and release the guilty—even if you are the one.

<u>Find and know Jesus the Christ for yourself.</u> It is impossible for anyone to do this quest for you. You will come to know Jesus Christ personally—individually. Apply His mercy to your life and being. He is life and can renew your will to live in God's purpose.

I John 1:9 clarifies the principle. "If we confess our sins, He is faithful and just to forgive us our sins, and cleanse us of all unrighteousness."

Purpose Driven Marriage

<u>Bible study and prayer will help you start again.</u> Ephesians 4:20-23 gives a plan to regain Godly purpose. "If indeed you have heard Him (Jesus) and have been taught by Him, as the truth is in Jesus: that you put off, concerning your former conduct, the old man which grows corrupt according to the deceitful lusts, and be renewed in the spirit of your mind (soul)."

<u>God's mercy reaches to you. It is essentially you find and decide to do marriage God's way</u>—that decision will produce results and good changes. "Put on the new man which was created according to God, in true righteousness and holiness." Ephesians 4:24 NKJ

<u>Peace can return, even after bitter separations.</u> Some marriages are raised from the dead at this point. Our healing can sometimes free a mate who is stuck in devilish bondage; or free us to rejoin a potentially great God begun marriage. Some, sad to say, are forever ended.

Summary:
- To avoid marriage ending in divorce should be a positive goal. There are often much causality because of the hurt to children and extended families. You continue to stay part of their lives through estranged. It is not a natural situation.
- Children often internalize that they are the cause of the whole problem. They can be severely damaged by fierce parental conflict and divorce.
- With God there is change and new seasons of life. Life does go on though you feel you are hanging somewhere and no one knows your plight.
- Jesus is the Lamb of God. His gift being applied to your life changes you.

- ➢ Simply put, step up to repent, regain purpose of God, Seek God's mercy and purity will flood your soul and you'll find the grace to forgive and forget about getting even.
- ➢ Know Jesus for yourself first!
- ➢ Bible study and regular prayer will help you start again.

Questions to Focus on Chapter 14 Insight:
1. What does divorce do to your support system?
2. Pretend you are a child and answer me, "Who is your grandma?"
3. What are some of the things God changes?
4. How was Jesus presented to the world the first, second and third time?
5. How do repenting and forgiving work together?
6. What steps can you take to restore God's Purpose to your life?

Chapter 15

Avoiding the Enduring Effects of Divorce

Embrace the seasons of Marriage—there must be mercy given and received. Life is like a vapor—it quickly vanishes. God has included life's seasons in His Purpose Driven Marriage. His purpose endures.

Seasons of marriage change with life's circumstances. The newlyweds give way to the parents. The parent stage gives way to the college age child leaving home—and the empty nest. The empty nest gives way to growing into senior adult times—of retirement or frustration of needing to work for financial reasons but without sufficient energy. Finally, we will face life without a beloved mate, or death for ourselves and leaving family here for the presence of God in the eternal realm. There are seasons of life—even beyond marriage problems.

Without purposeful forgiveness being extended, you will be unable to free yourself from the effects of change—terrible change—divorce. Some find it difficult to forgive personal failings which are perceived as leading to the divorce. In that case, first forgive yourself and your former

God's Purpose Drives A Marriage For A Lifetime

"one flesh" partner. God's purpose of forgiveness will free you from an unseen burden of the person and encourage a firm decision to never attempt to get even.

The bonds—if there is no hope for reconciliation—are best declared spiritually as well as legally broken. Now, you are responsible to God for yourself. Begin a time of prayer, Bible study and fasting requesting God's healing coupled with your repentance. Next include prayers for yourself and for your children's wounds. Children will have emotional and mental wounds. Consider them, please. Take time to listen and admit that they may have deep hurts too. Help them or get help for them.

If there is any hint of hope for reconciliation, seek the LORD. Lift yourself to the Lord first, then fast and pray for your estranged partner. Search out sources of help and do what you can to restore the marriage to health. It is better to mend a broken bond, than to limp through life with shattered emotions pulling your heart toward your former mate.

2 Kings 4 contains lots of miracles. God is still doing miracles. Seek miracles you need for your family as you read this and the following chapters. They will help with healing.

Genesis 26:1-12 tells how Isaac decided to do exactly what his father Abraham had done and illustrates the truth that families may follow the same sin pattern from one generation to the other. They both did their own thing and lied about their wives relationship to them. Their choices had national repercussions both times.

Purpose Driven Marriage

God is able to break sin cycles so that your children may follow God's purpose to drive their marriages for a life time.

God can change seasons—and does! Daniel 2:2-22 will help you see that God can work about you even in very difficult circumstances. Daniel, the eunuch was not allowed in the temple, prayed five times a day in his room and suffered persecution for finding strength from God. God does change seasons, and He will for you. Keep seeking His presence to change your season.

Face the FACT: Your partner who ended the difficult marriage may not change. That is not your problem. You must change—repent and go God's way. This will probably be the opposite way—or at least a great change, from the way you were going. Lets' say what if you continue opposing God's way? What could happen in the future is that you may set yourself up for yet another broken covenant. And, the pain because of it will again trouble your heart—even worse, your children's lives.

Some will realize, "I need help from outside council, now." Do seek help from a capable adult whom you trust, and know can listen with confidentiality. Skills can speedily bring help to aid you, so you can get through this problem without being judged.

The help usually will lessen the time it takes for pain to be touched and changed. It is also essential that you personally repent and begin following the purpose driven points of God's leading. His divine Hand can change all circumstances.

God's Purpose Drives A Marriage For A Lifetime

Remember God is faithful to help when you seek Him. Hebrews 11:6 "He is a rewarded of those who diligently seek Him."

Unfortunately, God's choices for people can be fouled up by our human choices. The choices often shock us as to how bad they are. They can determine that poor—less than divine purpose—destiny choices are selected by otherwise intelligent people. God never removed the free will He granted to His mankind. We may find that it is truly amazing grace God extends to us!

Again, the question: Can a poor choice for a marriage partner become our divine destiny?

Probably not! But, through prayer, fasting, dedication and one's diligent request for forgiveness for the "less than divine purpose driven choice"—then personal choices will at least become more strongly directed by God. This will predispose toward Godly blessings; and, pull us away from sticky problems caused by not first seeking God's purpose and wisdom for our marriage partner.

Some had very ungodly things happening in their bedrooms. How may choices change so that the marriage "bed" "coitus" is kept undefiled? Hebrews 13:4 "Marriage is honorable among all, and the bed undefiled; but fornicators and adulterers God will judge." In marriage God's purpose drives intimacy yet is to be maintained in a pure and holy way. Fleeing from the problems will require decisions for purity.

This also means that the many marriages which have entertained the cancer of 'porn' eating away at sexual purity—will need to change before marriage intimacy finally dies! Porn will totally kill any pure exchanges of intimacy. Partners will become totally defiled and sick inside. Please, study Section Two, Chapter 8 Intimacy for marriage saving suggestions before it is too late.

Determine to continue living in holiness with God's help.

An example of what can happen with God's help follows. The story starts with an obviously expectant wife begging for mercy from her husband. By God's mercy and grace, even after this child was conceived and born, and visibly not from the husband—not the husband's seed—a strong love and bonding was restored to the marriage.

You ask, "Could this really happen?"

My friend continued sharing. "Oh yes! God gave the grace we needed and our marriage is better now, than it ever had been. I'm totally forgiven, loved and restored. My child is totally loved too!"

My friend's eyes filled with tears of joy. " Mine did too! This can happen for you, if you can forgive yourself and others. God will work with you."

"Let no man separate that which God hath joined together, so they are no longer two but one." Matthew 19:6 NKJ

Prayer:
If you are wanting restoration here is a prayer to guide you. Let's pray.

Father God, Your plans are always the best. We've missed it. I need help and favor from Your storehouse of love to touch my estranged mate with this prayer. Grant me wisdom and compassion so that we may have a future together in line with Your purpose.

God's Purpose Drives A Marriage For A Lifetime

I've felt lots of emotions and need to have peace flood my heart and mind. Surround the children with Your arms of love and guard their hearts so they do not become bitter or resentful. Help me to become a better guide to Your heart and effectively show my love for them so they may feel secure.

When I feel unable to cope, lift me to Your presence and guide each thought and plan so that the end results will glorify You. I desire to please you and be pleasing in Your sight. Thank You for being real to my heart and bringing hope to me. Comfort my hurts and cause all grief and guilt to be changed and healed.

Most of all flood my heart with Your love, Lord Jesus. Thank You for forgiving my guilt before Your altar of holiness. Create in me a clean heart and renew a right spirit within me. Amen.

Summary:
- ➢ God's Purpose for Marriage and for our life both call us to embrace the changes in life. You are in the home—do your part. Get going!
- ➢ When a person is single—usually they sleep alone. If you have an ill child—maybe with feet in the face—you'll have some company for a couple of nights. Normal is sleeping alone!
- ➢ Single for whatever reason—needs to be faced. There are changes coming! Retirement and facing widowhood can also shock your constitution. Then, finally, like we faced this year, death calls, "Come, you've finished your course and kept the faith." And a life slips into eternal life with Jesus Christ! (Pastor/Dr. Grady left from Dr. Myrna's home May 31, 2009. He was 69 years in ministry. She'll relate the story of her personal start over that hap-

Purpose Driven Marriage

pened more than 30 years ago at the end of this chapter.)
- ➢ Hugs by your children are not as comforting as the presence of Jesus! Without Him you will feel lonely.
- ➢ In Christ's presence daily you'll find contentment and peace.
- ➢ God can change me so I can make it as a single person. He changes all the other things—surely I'm an easy work.
- ➢ Set your heart to rise to a new level of loving with God's kind of Agape' love. Seek grace and peace to dare to love without judging, selflessly, never out of order or in a fleshly way!
- ➢ Living life Driven by the Purposes of God is a total adventure. See you in Heaven and we'll discuss this for a couple of centuries when we know better what we're talking about. OK? Dr. M.

Questions to Focus on Chapter 15 Insight:
1. I don't like change, what can a body do?
2. Will God bless me even when I have flash backs and really detest that *.*?
3. Why is it best to change into line with the Purpose Driven Marriage?
4. How does human choice affect what God wants to do?
5. My marriage was not a God thing. What hope is there?
6. How can you KEEP a marriage bed pure and undefiled?
7. Did that story really happen—you know the forgiveness?
8. How many times should the Prayer for Restoration be prayed?

Chapter 16

The Grace to be Single or Begin Again

In conclusion, to begin again after marriage requires a TOTAL CHANGE of your thinking. There is NO ONE but you to move the furniture, cook breakfast, clean, earn the living, care for the children, go to the theater, or go out for a meal. You are again single! Only God can give you the grace to go on. Seek God's purpose each day for your life and family—from now on.

Get out of your chair; you will need to sleep in the bed— alone! Put a pillow beside you and tell Jesus you need His comforting presence. If you begin sleeping with the children at this time— you may have a terrible time getting back to a restful sleep time. They are hurting too, but are used to sleeping alone. Though you love them, face the truth, "I am single. Single people sleep ALONE! Only Jesus' love can comfort my heart even though the children can hug me."

God changes:

- Times
- Seasons
- Removes Kings
- Sets up Kings
- Gives Wisdom
- Gives Knowledge
- Reveals secret things

- Knows everything about you

God the Father sent Jesus, His saving lamb for you. Accept that He can change your heart and your life. Be comforted and ask for His grace for your life to become a blessing to others.

Though it is difficult, content yourself and seek God's peace for your mind. A scripture passage that comforted me was the chapter in I Corinthians 7:1-32. My prayer became: "God, change me so I'm contented, not seeking changes. Do, please, let me start over with You. This is Your day that You have made. I WILL rejoice and be glad in it! Amen."

This was loosely based upon one Psalm and Paul's request. Psalm 118:24 "This is the day which the LORD hath made; we will rejoice and be glad in it." And, Philippians 4:11 "In whatsoever state I am, therewith to be content." My life was to the observer, wonderful. But my purpose for life was nearly destroyed. The Holy Spirit began flooding my soul and baptized me with the fire of His glory!

He changes circumstances. Don't be surprised if your mountain of problems looks larger and darker than ever. Remember—just before DAY LIGHT BREAKS THROUGH is always the darkest time of the night! Keep looking for the morning when the peace comes!

Study 2 Kings 4:8-17 with an emphasis upon verse 14. Think MIRACLES! God will meet and deal with your needs in spectacular ways! (That's right, get your Bible and read the entire passage, please.)

BUT GOD! BUT GOD'S GRACE changes the darkness to the glory of the new day! The pain will be removed and His hand will comfort you as the circumstances change.

Content yourself and seek peace of mind. I Corinthians 7: 1-32 will help comfort and guide your thinking. Verse 27 admonishes: "Are you bound unto a wife/husband? Seek **not** to be loosed. Are you loosed from a wife/husband? Seek **not** a wife/husband…If you marry (For the reason study verse 9.), you have not sinned: and if a virgin marry, she has not sinned. Nevertheless such shall have trouble in the flesh."

Becoming content is very important. It will allow peace to surround you—no matter the other circumstances. The real world about you may be totally changing, and you can be comforted and contented by the Lord Jesus.

Rise to a new level of loving. **Love like God does.** He will grace you to do it.

Human affection when stretched, exercised and stressed may be pulled up to become divine love. Divine love originates with God—not with man. The result is that the human part of us is challenged to grow to the level of spiritual dimensions to be able to extend divine love. After 69 years—and finished counting May 31, 2009—in ministry, Dr. Grady Etheridge having attained Caleb's age (mountain taking age), was shown that Divine love can't be degraded to human affection after it has been graced to dwell in God's perspective. It becomes a love of self-Jesus-other without pulls or judgments.

You ask, "Can God's agape' love be reversed to fleshly affections? I doubt I can do this. Being single is not my favorite life."

The answer is:
NO! Divine love can't be degraded to Human affection. The reason is the spirit love is too pure to limit it to the fleshly confined level or to lower it to an out of order relationship.

This is a comforting revelation. Your body can be fasted into obedience to single living—if you will pay the price. You ask further: "Once the price is paid and single living can be maintained—can I do this with a sense of purity?"

The answer is:
YES! Continue to seek God's mercy for your life. He wants to help you. Do not faint in your mind. The grieving will be healed and your life will be able to be a blessing to the Lord, Jesus the Christ. Human life is very short. Eternity and God's purpose existence is forever in the presence of God. Seek His Grace! Following is a prayer to help restore your Godly purpose.

Remember, we can live driven by God's purpose; and, a Purpose Driven Marriage can last a life time. Following God's Holy purpose for marriage will always drive that marriage for a life time. Humans may fail, but God's purpose is eternally true.

God's Purpose Drives A Marriage For A Lifetime

Prayer to Restore His Purpose To Your Life

It is my heart's desire to begin again with You showing me the purpose for my life. At this time it seems lost in hurt and circumstances, but I am confident You are able to lead me step by step into Your purpose for my life. Help me to seek Your face each day. Guide me clearly as I study Your Holy Bible. Please, have the Holy Spirit give me understanding for each principle I am to follow. Take my hand, lead me, please.

The hurt and angers are laid at Your feet, Jesus. My heart is to begin a fresh start with Your leadership directing my life and family. Please, help me take care of my family, perform my daily tasks and keep courage for living. Draw my children toward You and help me guide them to godly life choices so they will have the fellowship with You to sustain their lives. Please, help them with their choices.

Now I realize that You direct us to the person who is best suited for the joint venture of marriage, and that without peace about the prospective partner there will be only struggles and problems. Since Your plan and purpose were set down in the scriptures, make me hungry to study each day. Help me plan use of my time so that I am able to accomplish Your desires. Place friends and spiritual help that is trustworthy into the path of my life.

Restore the sense of purpose to my heart. Be my comforter and savior. Restore peace and clarity within my thinking and will. I will thank You, Father God for the gift of Jesus the Christ and the guidance of the Holy Spirit. In Jesus' Name I pray, amen.

Purpose Driven Marriage

The Purpose Driven Marriage is one driven by God's purposes and easily can last a life time. Following God's holy purpose for marriage will always drive—literally propel—that marriage for an earthly life time. Humans may fail, but God's purpose is eternally true. Catch the vision of a joy filled marriage with strength, vigor and love that lasts and will be fondly remembered for eternity.

Summary:
- The primary unit of society is marriage. It is between a man and his wife.
- Marriage is the only blood covenant that is widely used in today's society and it is designed to last a lifetime.
- Healthy community depends upon healthy marriage.
- A husband to protect, provide for and tend to their wife to insure the continuation of mankind upon the earth. Without this support the woman would be in danger physically during pregnancy and during decision making times.

Questions to Focus on Chapter 16 Insight:
1. With change being such a part of life, can we ask God to help by giving us extra grace for the alterations?
2. When we realize we are single what are some things we can do to help get over the shock of living life solo?
3. Who is the only one able to really help comfort us?
4. How does God change the bleakness to a new outlook for life?
5. Do you dare to love folks who can't possibly help you back? Try it, you'll like it.
6. What miracle do you need in your life?

7. Is your body continuing to cry out for "action"? Tell it you'll starve it totally if it doesn't be quiet! Then begin some sort of fast to show your flesh you mean business.
8. Has God joined you to anyone beyond the bounds of a fleshly love for the sake of the ministry? (I hope so. Keep your flesh out of it. It far surpasses any limiting relationship.)

Dr. Grady Lloyd Etheridge, Ph.BD, DD.,MB, BA,

As you gathered Dr. Myrna is now a widow. When this book began September 2008 she and Dr. Grady expected to pass their 30th anniversary and perhaps more.

However, during the spring of 2009 Dr. Grady began a rapid decline in energy and by May 31, 2009 he passed to his eternal reward. It was quite a party for he spent 69 years in full time ministry and ministered in 31 nations of the world. Now his 32nd has been reached when he gained Heaven's portal.

He had much of the Bible memorized accurately and was very intelligent with nearly perfect recall of anything he read. Often his delightful humor perked up when the preaching needed relief. He was a really skilled and anointed preacher. He founded 18 churches and two Bible Colleges. His work showed the apostle's anointing.

For twenty-nine years and 11 months Dr. Grady was husband to Dr. Myrna in God's Purpose Driven Marriage. Dr. Myrna had been badly tested by deaths of two sons with cystic fibrosis and marriage failure—the awful word—DIVORCE! To wear divorce was an awful sign in the Christian world—worse than Bubonic Plague would have been!

She knew she was called to full time ministry since the age of 12—in a Billy Graham meeting in St. Louis, MO, but had never seen how a Baptist woman could minister—other than be a missionary. She ministered at 17 years of age with a revival team in week long revivals and many weekend meetings.

She lived on the mission field for 6 years and helped with whatever needed to be done in her church home in Puerto Rico. Her sons' father left and the divorce was final several months later. She felt clear of most of the guilt but lamented greatly over the broken covenant.

There in Puerto Rico she received the Baptism with the Holy Spirit and the call came alive again in her heart. Much happened that wasn't worth writing about, but the prayer times increased dramatically.

Her personality changed so much that her best friend asked, "Are you the same Myrna? You are so happy and laughing. It was bad, wasn't it?" Myrna didn't answer—she determined there was no real benefit. She has prayed.

Work out of the country ended for her and she returned home. And later, back in her family home town, she began fasting for extended periods of time—as long as 21 days on water with a little juice. God began talking to her about writing. She began her first book an autobiography titled "Momma, What's It Like to Die?"[3] She pleaded with the Lord to set her free and cleanse her life and allow her to start over. She prayed this way for over two years. She was dyslexic, severely allergic and had symptoms of cystic fibrosis too. (Several years into marriage the deliverances and healings manifested.)

---

3. *Momma, What's It Like to Die?* By Myrna L. Goehri Etheridge, 1984,1985,1999 Treasure House An Imprint of Destiny Image, ISBN 1-56043-331-0 available from local book seller or www.reapernet.com

Purpose Driven Marriage

The writing opened all the infected scars of the hurts of the loss of two sons she adored along with the stigma of the divorce she hated as much as God did. Mourning she had never faced surfaced. She cried so much that her face began to look like death.

The repenting went on and on. Finally, without a place to live or very much cash she was called into her Dad's office. Her Dad made the writing happen by making her an offer she couldn't refuse. She was earning a living mowing 35 acres of a mobile home court her family managed. Writing inside, mowing outside she passed the days. It worked fine! (Sand burrs are awful!)

A local pastor was in the post office the same time as Myrna—getting mail from PO Box 564—like she has for 35 years. He had been crying too—she told him to talk with her mother (His long time Summer Camp helper.) and she'd pray for him. He said, "ok, I will." She left and prayed, "Lord, do something for that man. He can't hear; his wife died two months ago; his daughter is having bad problems; and, his sister-in-law may have cancer." She had no idea she was to be in God's Purpose Driven Marriage with him for nearly 30 years! He began circling the mobile home court as she mowed.

One day He showed up at Dr. Myrna's home and the rest is history. No dating, No courting—they knew it was God's Purpose Driven Marriage. He was 15 years her elder. The town gossips had grossly overrated lots of details, but Dr. Grady decided they were to marry after not seeing her since the week after the Post Office encounter.

A few days past six months from that day post office encounter, January 16, 1979, they were getting a blood test for marriage. June 30th, 1979 at 6 p.m. they were married

God's Purpose Drives A Marriage For A Lifetime

in a simple ceremony in Dr. Myrna's parent's front room. It's been quite a trip!

Within six weeks of marriage, just after they moved into the second home he had ever owned, Dr. Grady yelled out—while circling their kitchen in the middle home—"I can't stay with you, I'll be making you commit adultery." With a few more circles—he left the home very upset. Dr. Myrna's greatest fear was he would leave.

Half crying, half shouting, Dr. Myrna loudly reminded the Lord, "God, you said what you have joined together not to let any man put asunder. By the power of Jesus' Name I send angels out to call Grady Etheridge back into his home. In Jesus' Name I constrain him—come home." She continued in tongues—than repeating this simple prayer with heartfelt emotions.

About 30 minutes later—he returned home. His head in his hand he was saying sadly, "I don't know what got into me, I can't leave you. I love you too much."

This happened several other times—with the same return and lack of understanding of the scripture which is so clearly written. Check Matthew 5:32; 19:9; Mark 10:11 and Luke 16:18. Oh, thank you Jesus for a new and better blood covenant that cleanses sin.

The Lord Jesus sent a dear singer/preacher, Mike Adkins, to be guest in their church. Dr. Grady told Bro Mike about thinking that Dr. Myrna was being caused to commit adultery… Bro. Mike was an angel from God. He asked a simple question. If you are doing this sin, then God couldn't bless you, could He? Answer is NO.

Purpose Driven Marriage

But God was blessing. The ministry team for G & M Etheridge Min., Inc. had reached to China and the now Premier of China with an open vision telling Dr. Grady each thing to share around the table for twelve. Dr. Grady was with Neil Armstrong taking the flag from the moon to China. They witnessed openly to the officials for two hours in Beijing, May 1983. . They pastored a church and then helped begin a church that mushroomed to 150 in a few months. They've been hours on Christian TV, both TBN and TCT. The first book was published and during that time they pastored another church in California and God sent Dr. Grady to the Holy Land. Since the Purpose Driven Marriage was founded in 1979 there are three new churches and a college that reaches 102 nations, 15,000 or more students in 1,500 plus teaching locations (The number changes all the time.) with Bible curriculum in two languages and pieces in 6 other languages. There are now 11 books and one recording of songs the Lord has given Dr. Myrna. They both served as elders in their home church, Christ Church of the Heartland until Dr. Grady went home May 31, 2009. He was a guest on Total Christ Television in March of 2009 and preached his last sermon on April 12, 2009. He wasn't sick. He just changed residences! He finished his course. Dr. Myrna is staying before the Lord daily and living a fasted life. He is faithful.

Jesus' blood covers all sin when we truly repent and He changes our life to His ways to complete His purposes and plans for our lives.

When this book began Dr. Myrna had no idea this type of change was so close in her own life.

Dear Reader, Yes, lots of things are different, but in all things, It is well with my soul. Jesus resides in my heart in a real and meaningful presence. It is well! Thanks for reading and seeing my heart. There is hope. Don't forget Jesus' blood is perfect redemption.

ABOUT THE AUTHORS

Dr. Paul Obadare, Ph.D., Dr. C, SCC, MRS, BA in Religious Studies

Dr. Paul Obadare called and gifted as teacher and healing evangelist coupled with years of counseling experience and much study has captured the divine purpose for marriage in this writing. That purpose will drive successful marriages, thus Purpose Driven Marriage came into existence.

Dr. Paul, born, in Ilesha, Nigeria, West Africa is the first son of Dr., Apostle T.O. Obadare. Guided by his father, widely revered television-evangelist who founded WOSEM worldwide, Dr. Paul sought the Lord for his own anointing since an early age. Formal ministry began in 1982 as student pastor with World Soul Winning Evangelistic Ministry, International. His life is one of prayer and fasting.

Becoming the first Africa minister in 1986 at Mount Zion Primitive Baptist church in Selma Alabama, he served as the associate minister during his student years at Selma University. After graduation in 1987 with his BA in Religious Studies he completed a Master of Religious Studies at Howard University Divinity School, Washington D.C. A Ph.D., in Theology from International Seminary in Florida, USA was completed in 1992. Maple Springs Baptist College and Seminary, Capital Heights, Maryland USA awarded Dr. Paul Obadare a Doctorial degree in counseling in 1996. In 2008 the Satisfied Christian

God's Purpose Drives A Marriage For A Lifetime

Counselor, SCC, was awarded by AACC from Virginia. At Maple Springs he served as a Professor of New Testament for 7 years, and started WOSEM Bible College in 2004. He served as President of WOSEM Bible College and Seminary in Maryland, USA. After the BA he married his lovely wife and they have four gifted children. And now he leads and oversees WOSEM world-wide. Great favor flows to him from God and people.

He will ably guide you to think deeply revealing how God's purpose was for the joy and completion of your marriage bringing more happiness and peace than you thought possible—one letter-word at a time. Share this book with your friends so they will understand how to carry on a <u>Purpose Driven Marriage</u>. Joy and happiness are to be part of your marriage.

Dr. Myrna L. Etheridge, Ph.D., D.D., D.D., MSE, BSE

Dr. Myrna teaches and ministers for many organizations and churches. Ministry has taken her to 32 nations of the world. Ministry in Nigeria has brought her to friendship with WOSEM and its officials since 2006. Myrna travels thousands of miles while conducting seminars, preaching, or leading in music worship (instrumental or singing). She and Dr. Grady were married 30 years and often ministered together. She serves as elder in her home church, Christ Church of the Heartland. Much time is invested in ministry to individuals, often in the area of marriage relationships.

Myrna was reared on a small farm near St. Louis, MO. While driving a tractor as a ten year old farmer's daughter she learned to love the earth and the life it brings forth. She has done much "field" study since then. Called into ministry at age 12 she served in her local church in many different capacities, teaching, helping, musician, and whatever needed doing. Within four months of each other both of Myrna's sons died with the hereditary disease, Cystic Fibrosis. Shortly after that her marriage failed. This work contains important lessons she learned from these heart breaking experiences. During this time she was troubled with her own symptoms of Cystic Fibrosis. Myrna sought the LORD for answers to why anyone must suffer so. The LORD began to teach Myrna, step by step about living in freedom from genetic diseases and problems. Today she is free of the genetic problems. Divorced persons will find much help and comfort to carry on with life and deepen their fellowship with the Lord Jesus.

Professionally Dr. Myrna taught 18 years in public schools and college in USA and Puerto Rico. She has often been a program guest on local and national TNB and TCT Christian Television. She's a home-town girl called to serve Jesus with added international flavor. She earned BSE and MSE degrees in Biology 1964-65 from Arkansas State University, USA. The 1990 Ph.D.in Systematic Theology is from Channel Cities Christian College, Ventura, CA; and, she has received two D.D. Degrees. She has taught Bible on Collegiate level. Since 1984 she has authored nine books (three others with Dr. Paul). Myrna has served on mission tours to 32 nations including Haiti, Honduras, Puerto Rico, Panama, Nigeria, Ghana, South Africa, London, Europe, etc. She is listed in Who's Who in Leaders of Science Ed. 1967-68 and eleven other Who's Who volumes. Her books and information are available when you visit http://www.gmeministries.org, your favorite book seller or www.authorhouse.com .

COMBINED BENEFITS OF THE AUTHORS

Where can you find **Purpose Driven Marriage** explained better than by two diverse persons like Paul Obadare and Myrna Etheridge?

Purpose Driven Marriage is presented from rich ethnic backgrounds of a Nigerian African, Southern USA, and English values combined with a northerner who is part Cherokee Indian as well as USA farm grown German and French.

Both authors are doctored several times with rich experiences in Bible study, fasting, ministry and marriage graced with strong Christian family backgrounds encompassing the world. Their combined ministry years are pushing 100. Pastor/Dr. Paul lives in London, UK. Dr. Myrna lives in the heartland of USA. Both spend many hours counseling, praying and helping those with troubled, failing, or ending marriages. Here is help. You are looking at the right book. They teamed up for your benefit.

Reading and studying this book will reveal much insight as to why the combination of the years of individual fasting, study and experience of Rev./Dr. Paul Obadare and Rev./Dr. Myrna Etheridge is so vital to the **Purpose Driven Marriage** and your marital happiness.

Living a vital Christian life with signs and wonders following is of utmost importance to both the authors. Eternal life is through Jesus' death on the Cross of Calvary and the resurrected Christ's powerful victory. God, in His wisdom sets the appointment opportunities within each marriage relationship. Listening for His leading is vital to gaining the effective, loving outreach of the Purpose Driven Marriage.

You can mature and develop a **_Purpose Driven Marriage. God's Purpose Drives Marriage for a Life Time_**. Be sure you get your copy today from your favorite book seller or www.authorhouse.com!

Made in the USA
Lexington, KY
16 May 2011